AF594415

THE *Little Book of* PEGGYS COVE & THE SOUTH SHORE

LEN WAGG

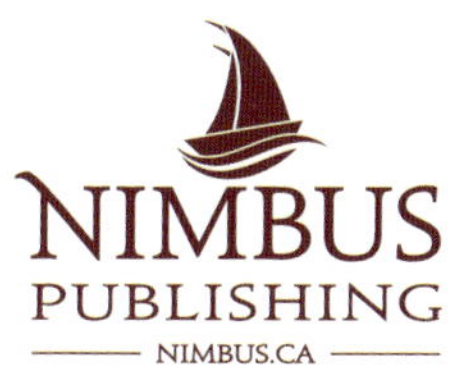

THANKS TO ALL WHO HELPED ME ALONG MY JOURNEY BY LETTING ME ONTO THEIR PROPERTIES, BY GIVING ME DIRECTIONS, AND BY LETTING ME KNOW WHERE THEIR OWN "BEST SPOTS" ARE.

AS ALWAYS, THANKS TO SANDY WAGG FOR ALL HER HELP ALONG THE WAY.

Nimbus Publishing Limited
3660 Strawberry Hill Street, Halifax, NS, B3K 5A9
(902) 455-4286 nimbus.ca

Printed and bound in China

NB1513

Editor: Angela Mombourquette
Design: Jenn Embree

Library and Archives Canada Cataloguing in Publication

Title: The little book of Peggys Cove & the South Shore / Len Wagg.
Other titles: Little book of Peggys Cove and the South Shore | Peggy's Cove & the South Shore
Names: Wagg, Len, author.
Identifiers: Canadiana 20200172689 | ISBN 9781771088213 (hardcover)
Subjects: LCSH: Peggys Cove (N.S.)—Pictorial works. | LCSH: Nova Scotia—Pictorial works.
Classification: LCC FC2349.P45 W34 2020 | DDC 971.6/2050222—dc23

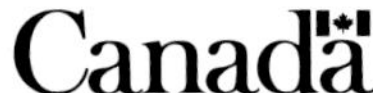

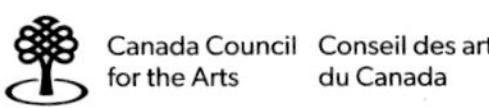

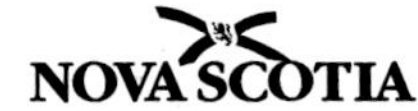

Nimbus Publishing acknowledges the financial support for its publishing activities from the Government of Canada, the Canada Council for the Arts, and from the Province of Nova Scotia. We are pleased to work in partnership with the Province of Nova Scotia to develop and promote our creative industries for the benefit of all Nova Scotians.

Introduction

THE CLOUDS DARKEN FROM FAINT TO VIBRANT RASPBERRY sherbet as dawn approaches. At first, the red cap of Peggys Point Lighthouse pops with colour, and then the pinkish sunlight works its way down the white lighthouse as the sun rises above the horizon. The granite glimmers in the early morning light as it has for thousands of years, since the ice age stripped off the topsoil.

It's dawn at Peggys Cove, and it's spectacular.

From the nearby cove, the sound of a diesel engine precedes the sight of a small Cape Islander boat heading out for a day's work. Working on the sea is integral to this community; in fact, it's integral to every community along the South Shore of Nova Scotia. From the earliest days of the Mi'kmaq, the ocean and its bounty have been part of everyday life here.

The waves, as they do twenty-four hours a day, crash against the unyielding stone. Some days—like during hurricane season—the waves crash far above the normal high-tide marks. In extreme storms, the sea can suck roads, buildings, and trees out with it.

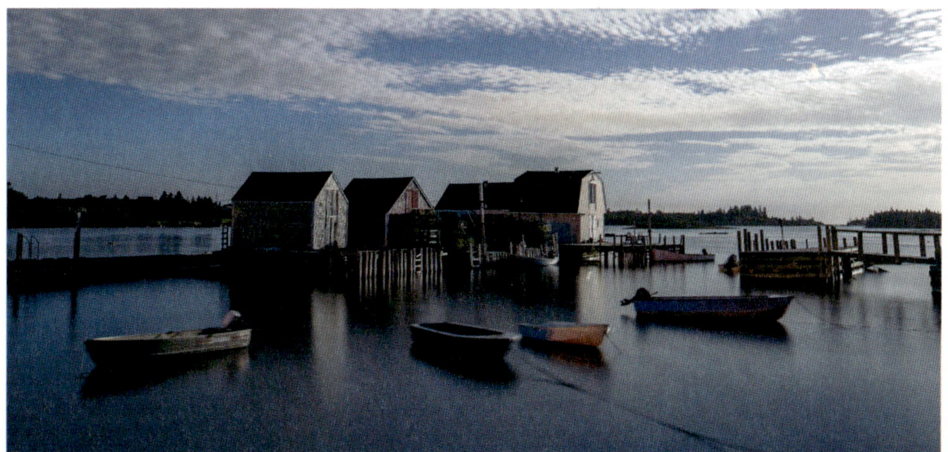

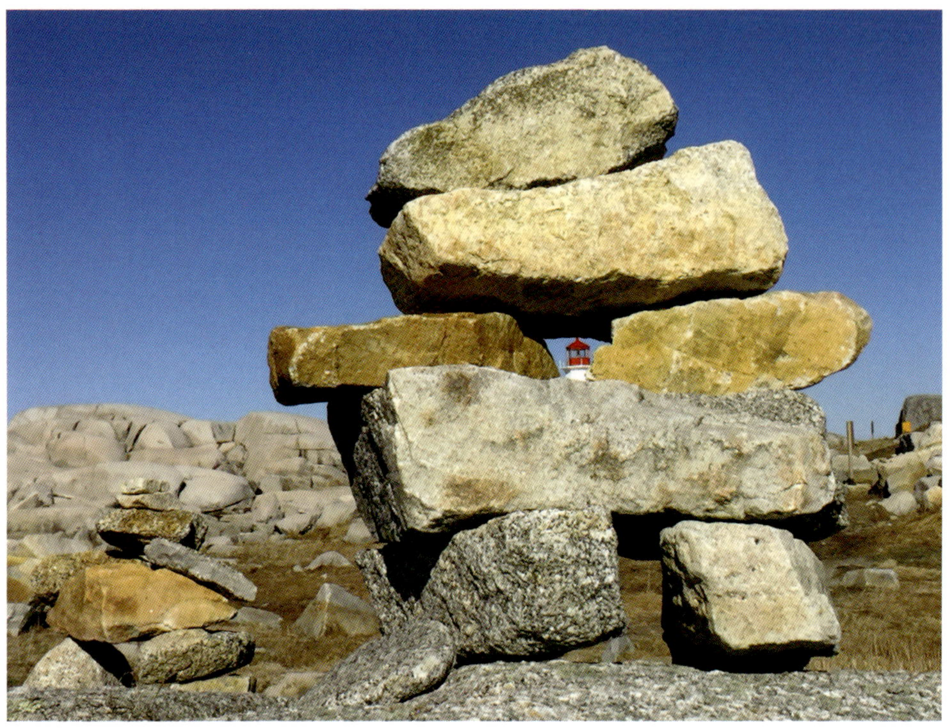

Farther south, boats find refuge in harbours and inlets all along the shore. Any turn of a road might reveal a ship anchored in a mirror-calm cove.

Lunenburg, with its storied shipbuilding past, is the present-day home of Nova Scotia's famed sailing ambassador, *Bluenose II*. The majestic schooner can be seen tied up at its berth during the winter months, or sailing around the province in the summertime. Visitors have the chance to talk to the crew and get a sense of what life was like on board for those who earned a living from the sea.

Other communities along the South Shore are peppered with unique architecture and majestic homes that face out to sea. And whether you're wandering the annual Scarecrow Festival in Mahone Bay or enjoying the summertime tradition of sipping a drink and watching the yachts go by during Chester Race Week, there's a year-round event to suit every visitor.

Sometimes, the end of a dirt road reveals a crescent of white sand and sparkling aquamarine water. The beauty of a beach on Nova Scotia's South Shore is

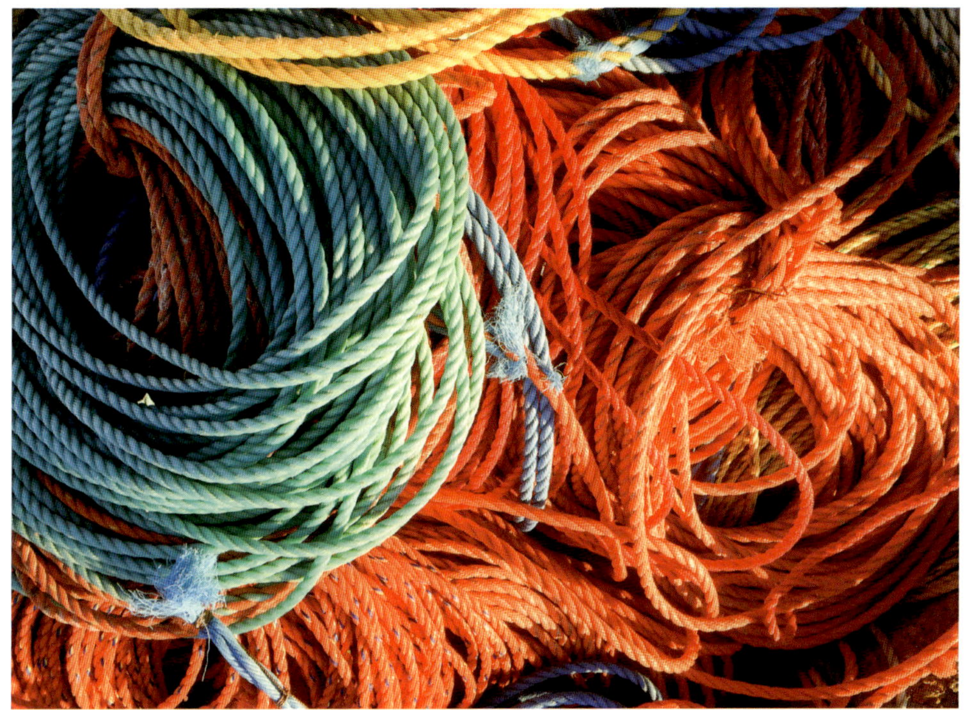

not just in the scenery; often, you can have the whole place to yourself. It's easy to lose a whole day with a book and a blanket.

Island-hopping across bridges in the Tusket Islands area reveals the vibrant Acadian culture—and it is alive and well. That iconic combination—red, blue, white, and the gold star—is everywhere.

Driving into Yarmouth you can see the shops along the main street that reflect the historic past of this port community and its ties to the sea. Every November, at the tip of Cape Forchu, one can experience Dumping Day: the opening of the rich lobster grounds for the season. Standing on the rocks in the dark, shoulder-to-shoulder with hundreds of other people, you hear the rumbling engines of hundreds of boats as they make their way past the lighthouse. This annual tradition of wishing the fishers well—horns blaring, people waving, and flashlights and torches lighting the sky—reminds us that the South Shore of this province, its people, and the ocean are all tied together in a relationship that has remained strong for thousands of years.

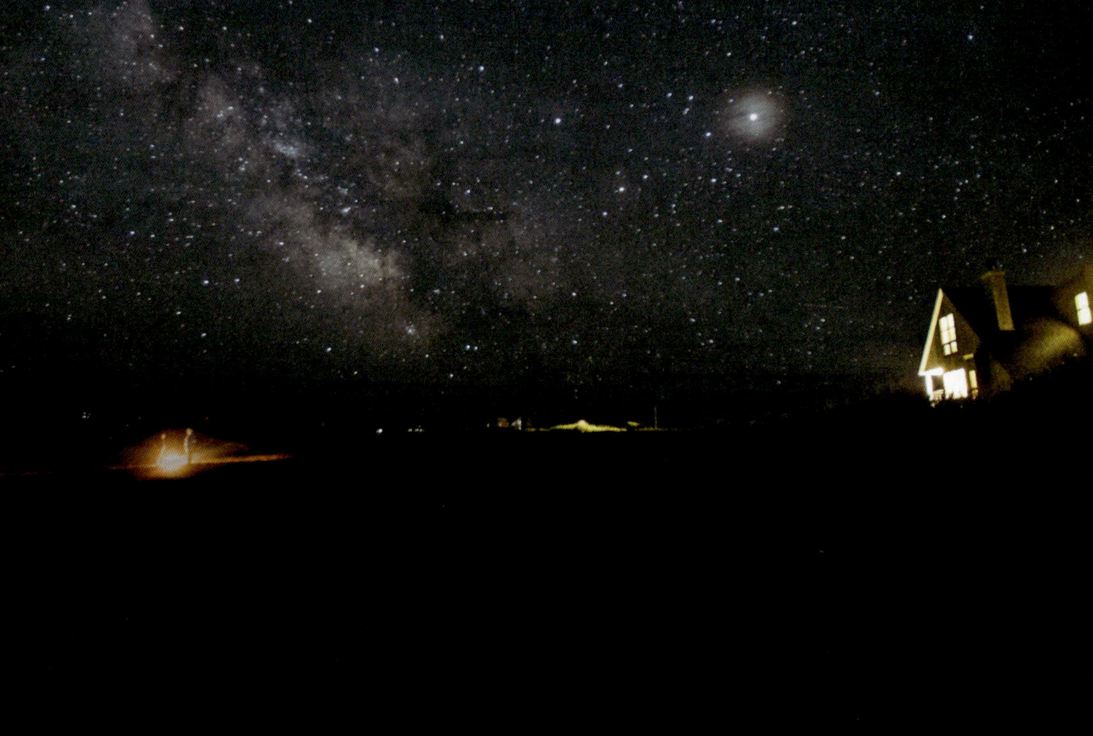

ABOVE ⁓ Friends enjoy a campfire on Kingsburg Beach as the Milky Way and planets roll across the August night sky.

FACING ⁓ The International Space Station, its reflective solar panels shining bright, makes its transit over the Peggys Point Lighthouse in this long exposure, taken on a winter night.

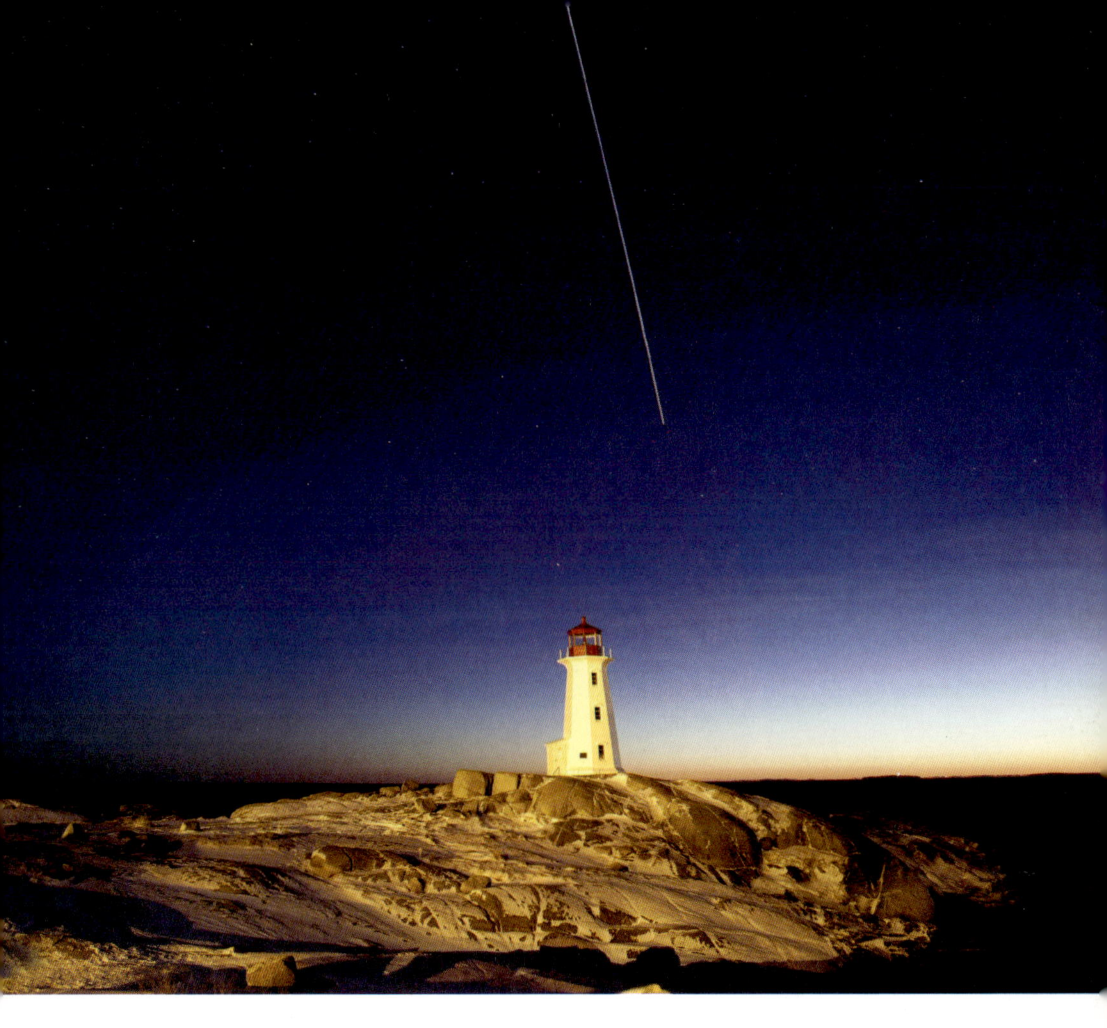

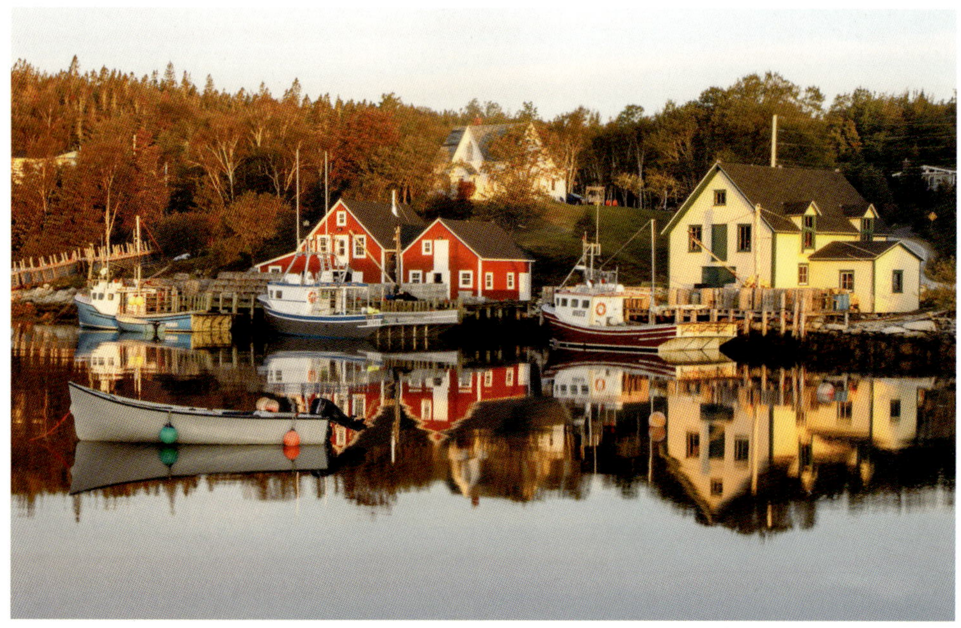

ABOVE ⁓ The early morning sun bathes the tiny community of Northwest Cove on the shores of St. Margarets Bay in an orange light.

FACING ⁓ A piping plover gathers her brood around her on a South Shore beach. The tiny birds nest on the shores of Nova Scotia.

OVERLEAF ⁓ The rising sun reveals a mist that floats above the waves at Bayswater Beach on the Aspotogan Peninsula.

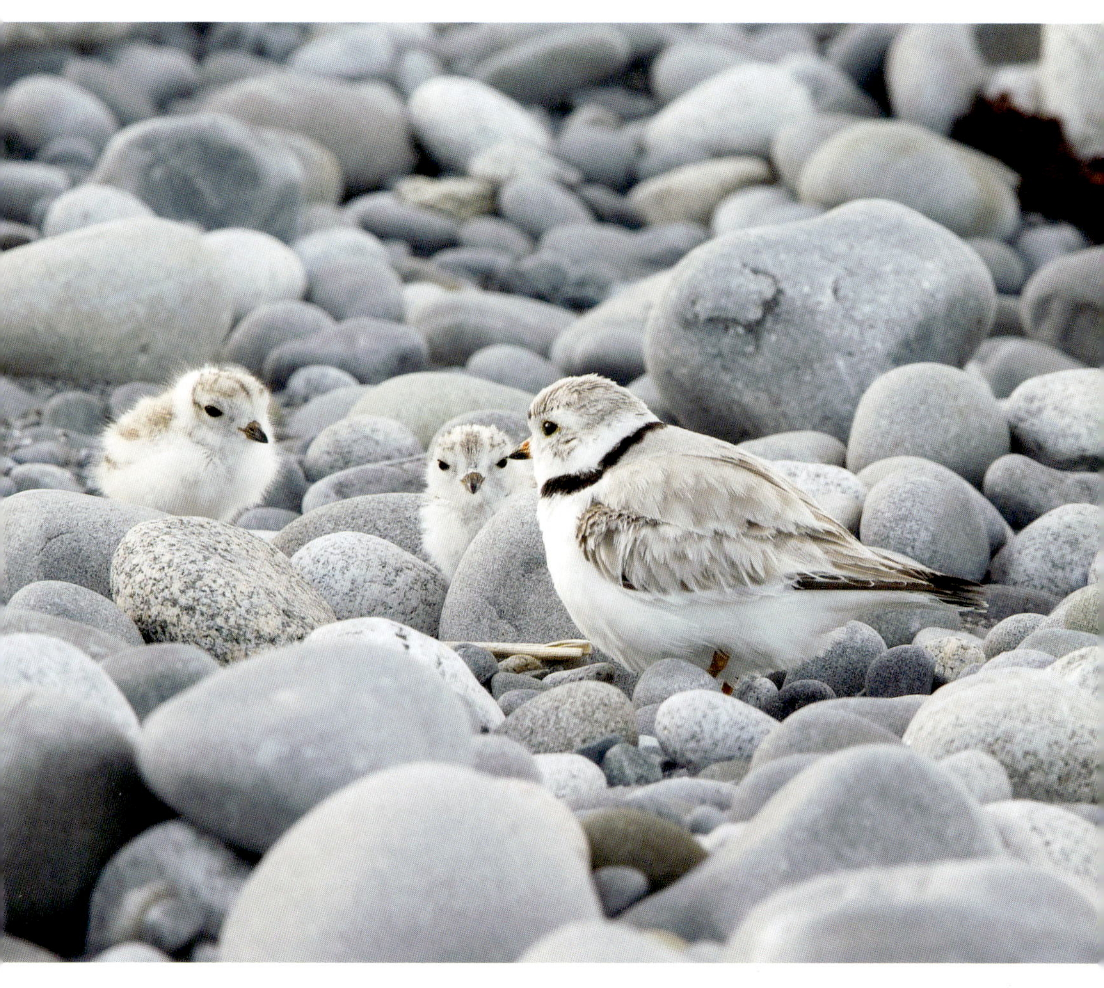

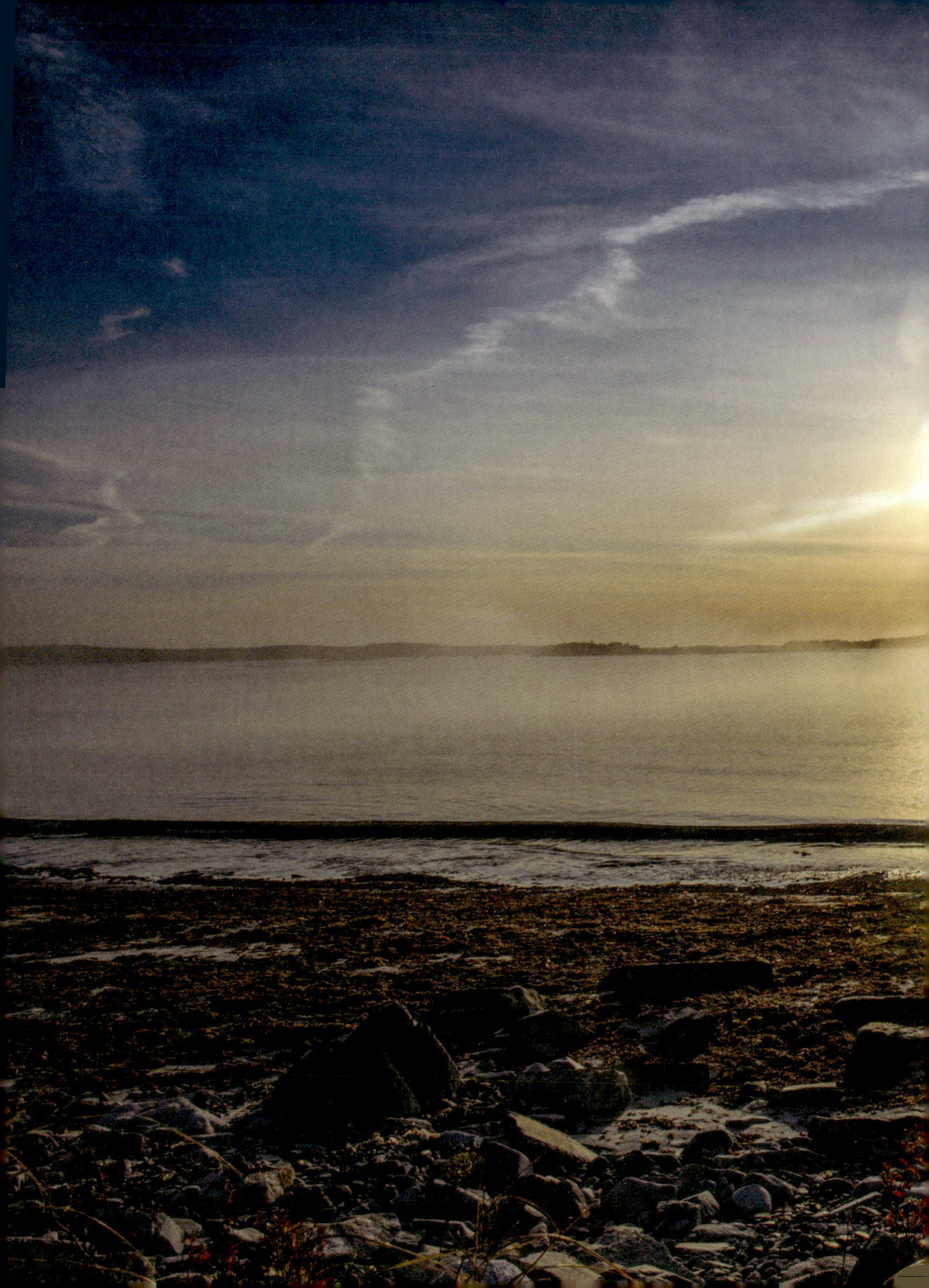

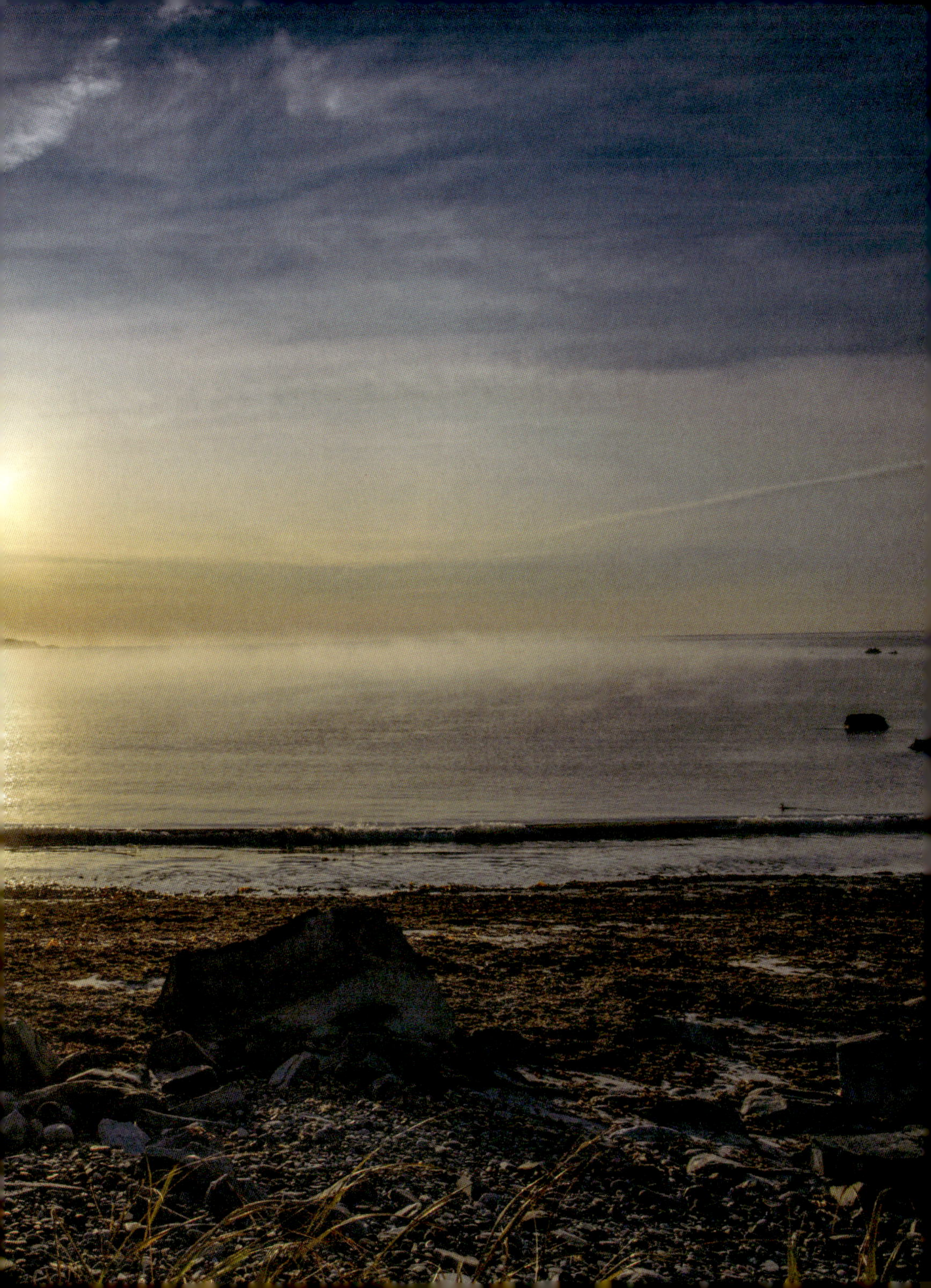

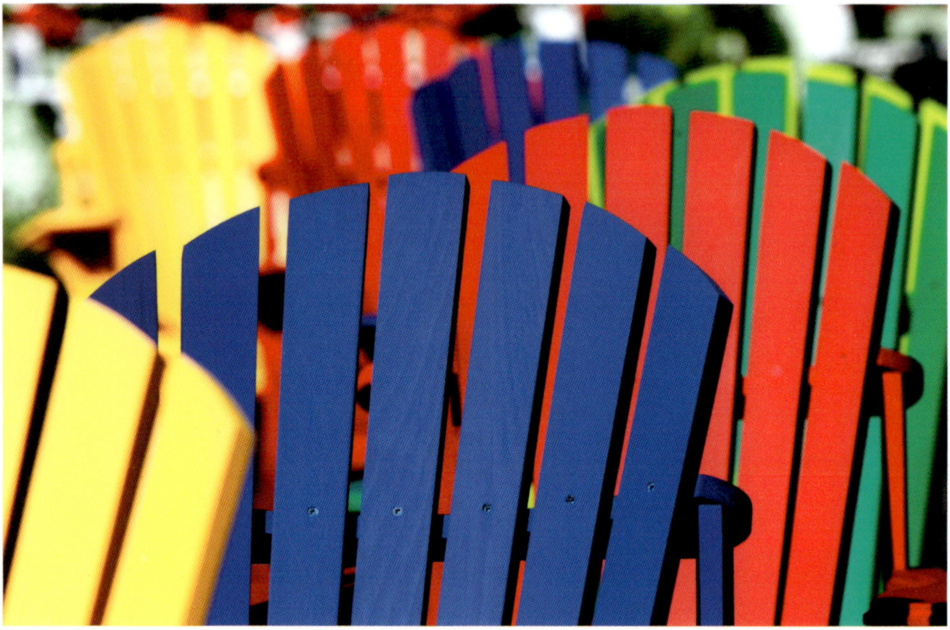

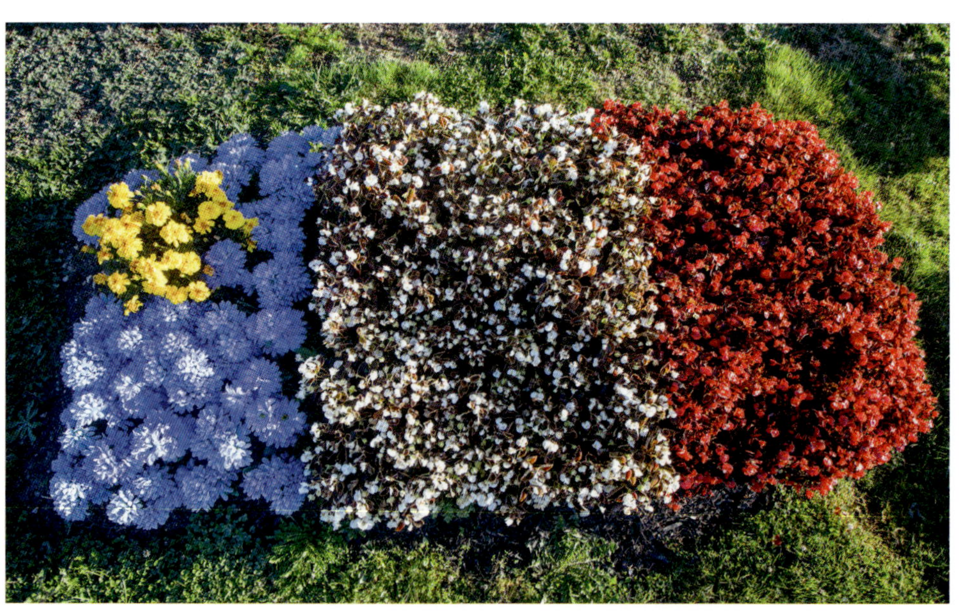

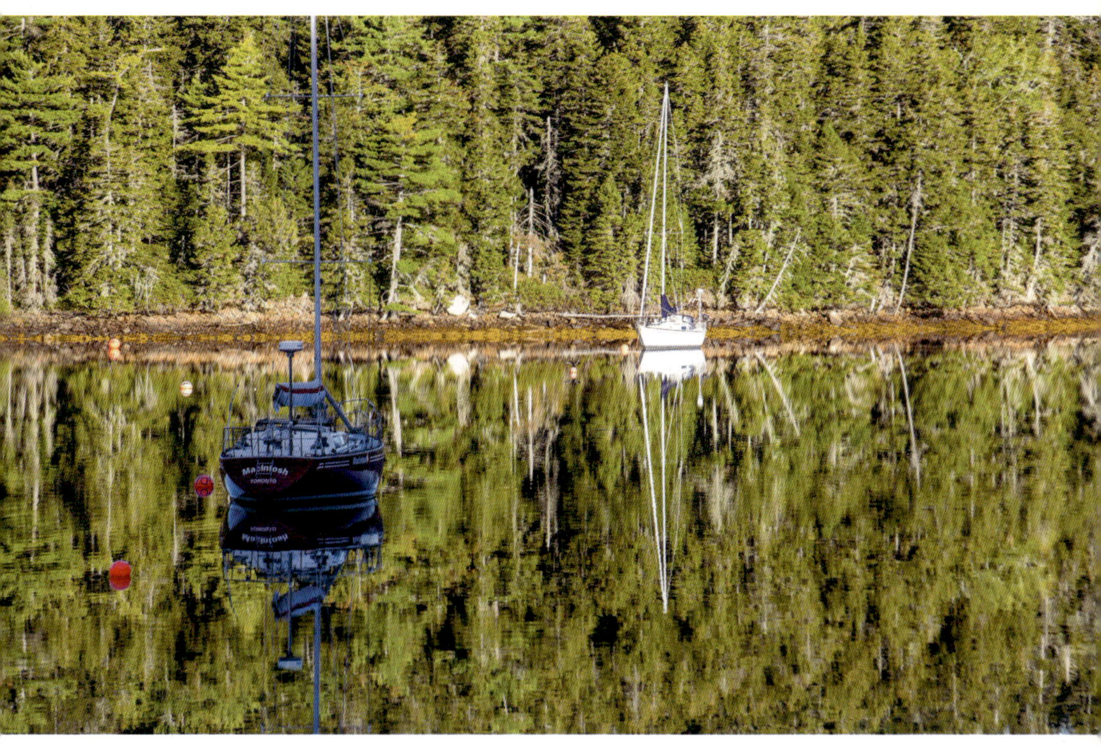

ABOVE ⁓ Dawn at Deep Cove, Aspotogan Peninsula.

FACING ABOVE ⁓ These colourful deck chairs can be seen at cottages and homes all over Nova Scotia.

FACING BELOW ⁓ A flower bed, created in the colours of the Acadian flag, welcomes visitors to the Historic Acadian Village in Lower West Pubnico.

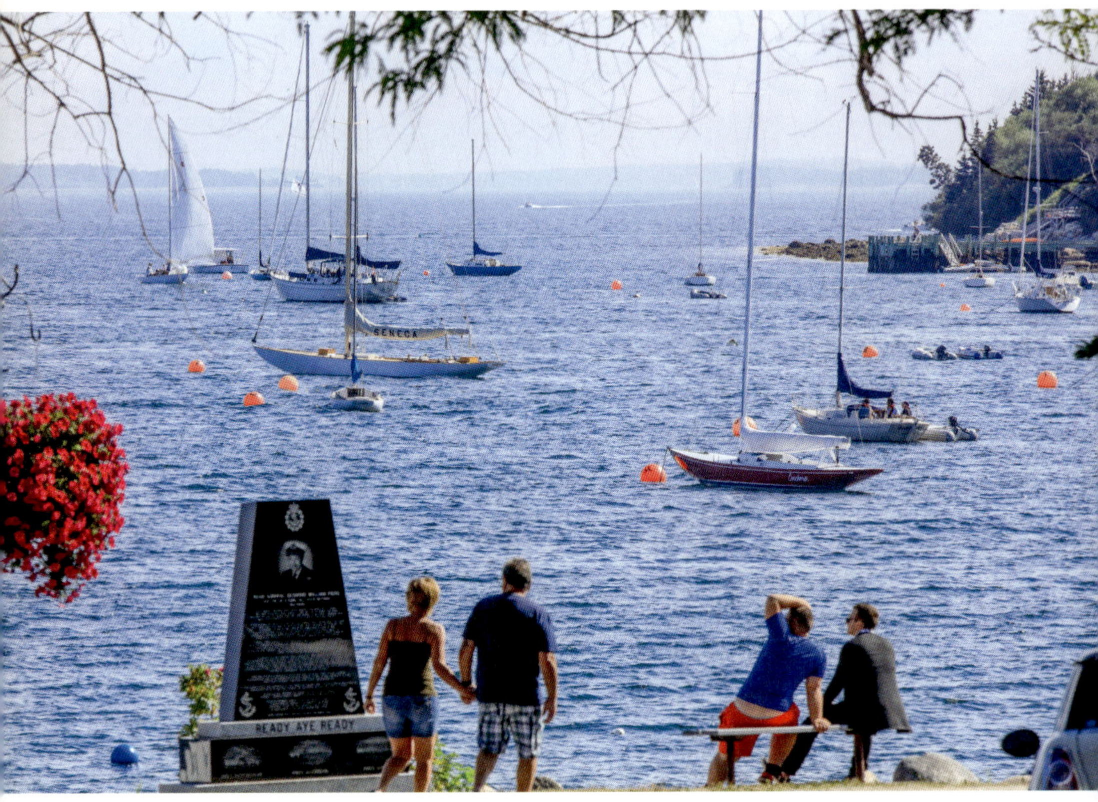

ABOVE ∾ Spectators gather for Chester Race Week, which is in full swing during the third week of August. For 150 years, races that bring boats from all over Nova Scotia have been held in the seaside community.

FACING ∾ Nova Scotia's tallest lighthouse, at 101 feet, sits at Cape Sable on Cape Sable Island. The Mi'kmaw name for the island is Kespoogwitik.

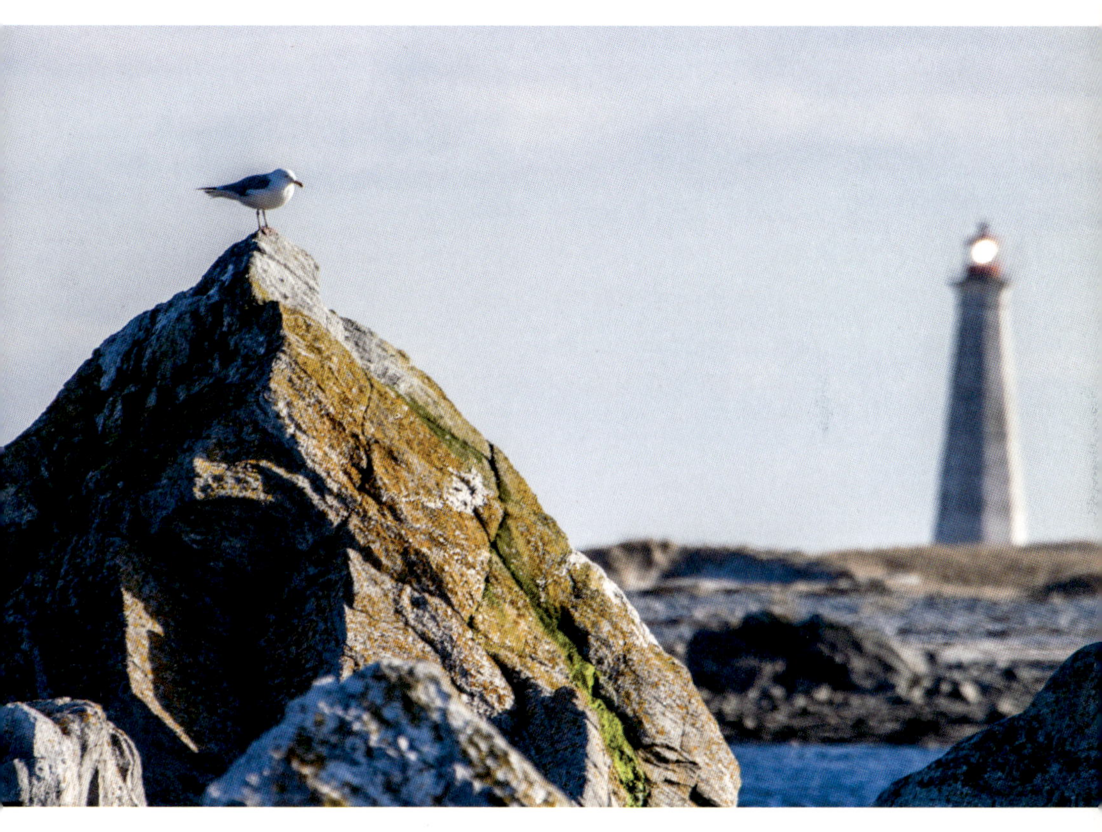

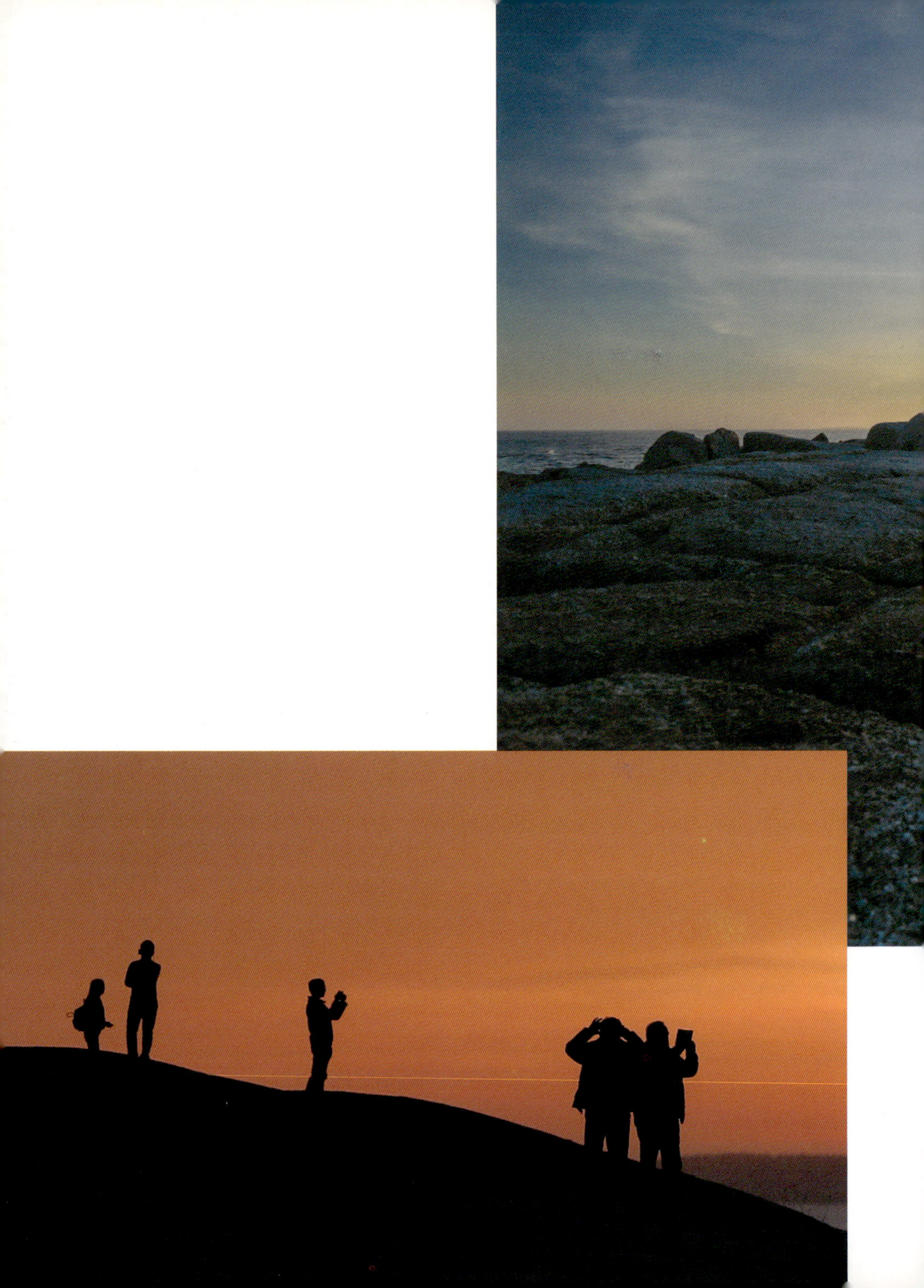

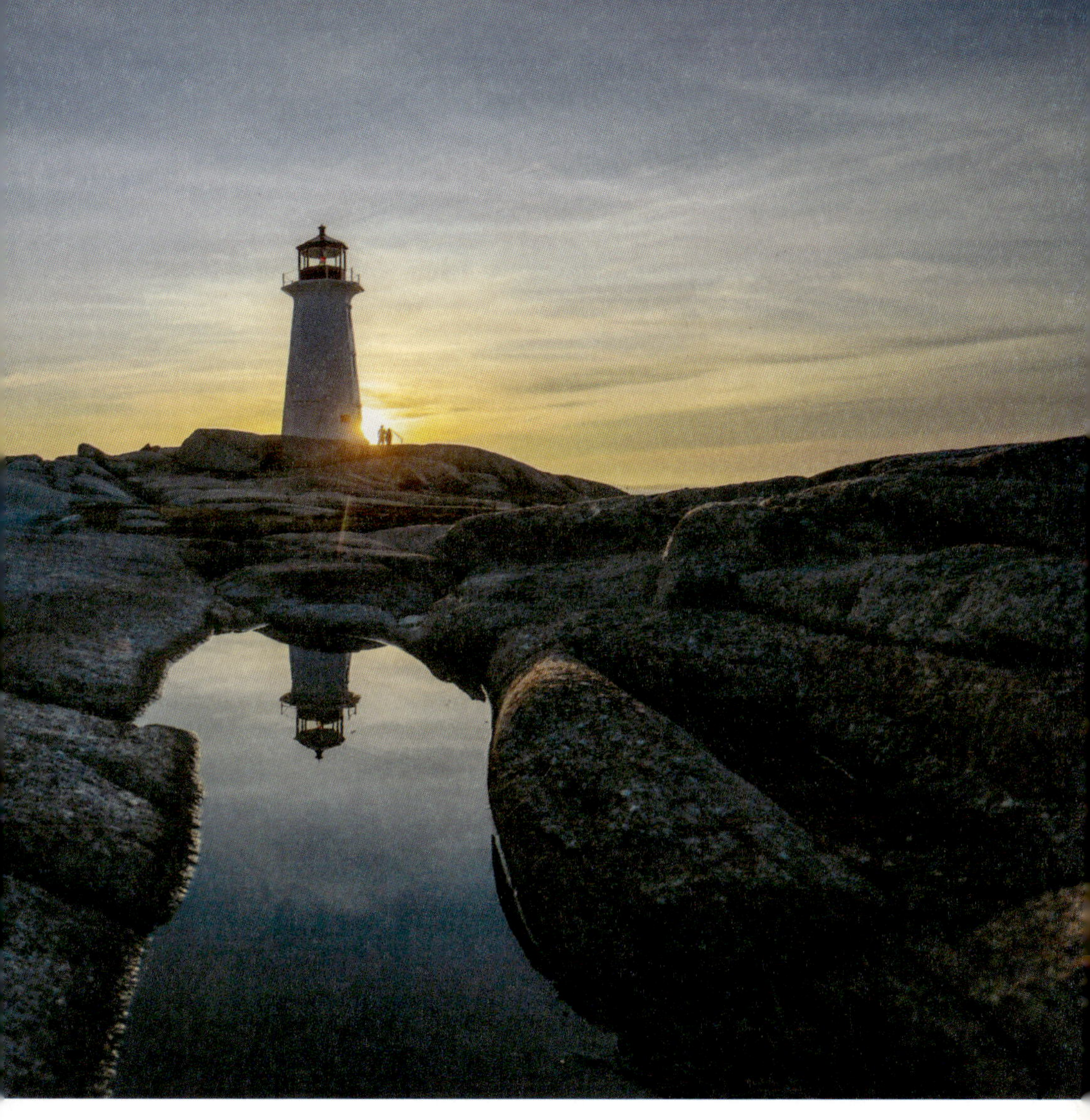

ABOVE ⁓ The sun sets behind the Peggys Point Lighthouse as photographers and tourists enjoy the scene.

FACING ⁓ Visitors take in the fading light of the setting sun along the rocks at Peggys Point.

OVERLEAF ⁓ The rising sun glows behind one of Nova Scotia's first wind farms, built in 2005 at Pubnico Point.

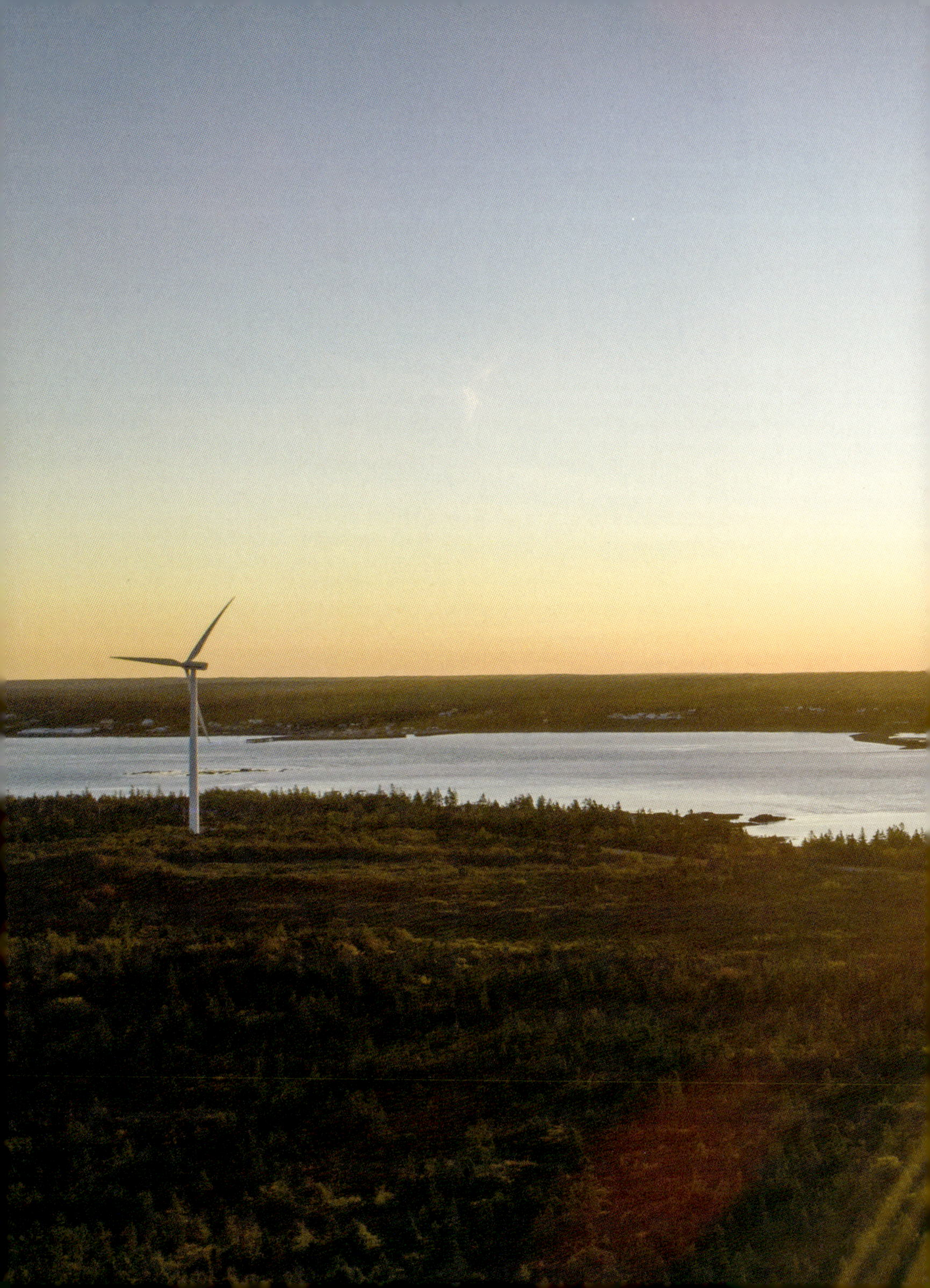

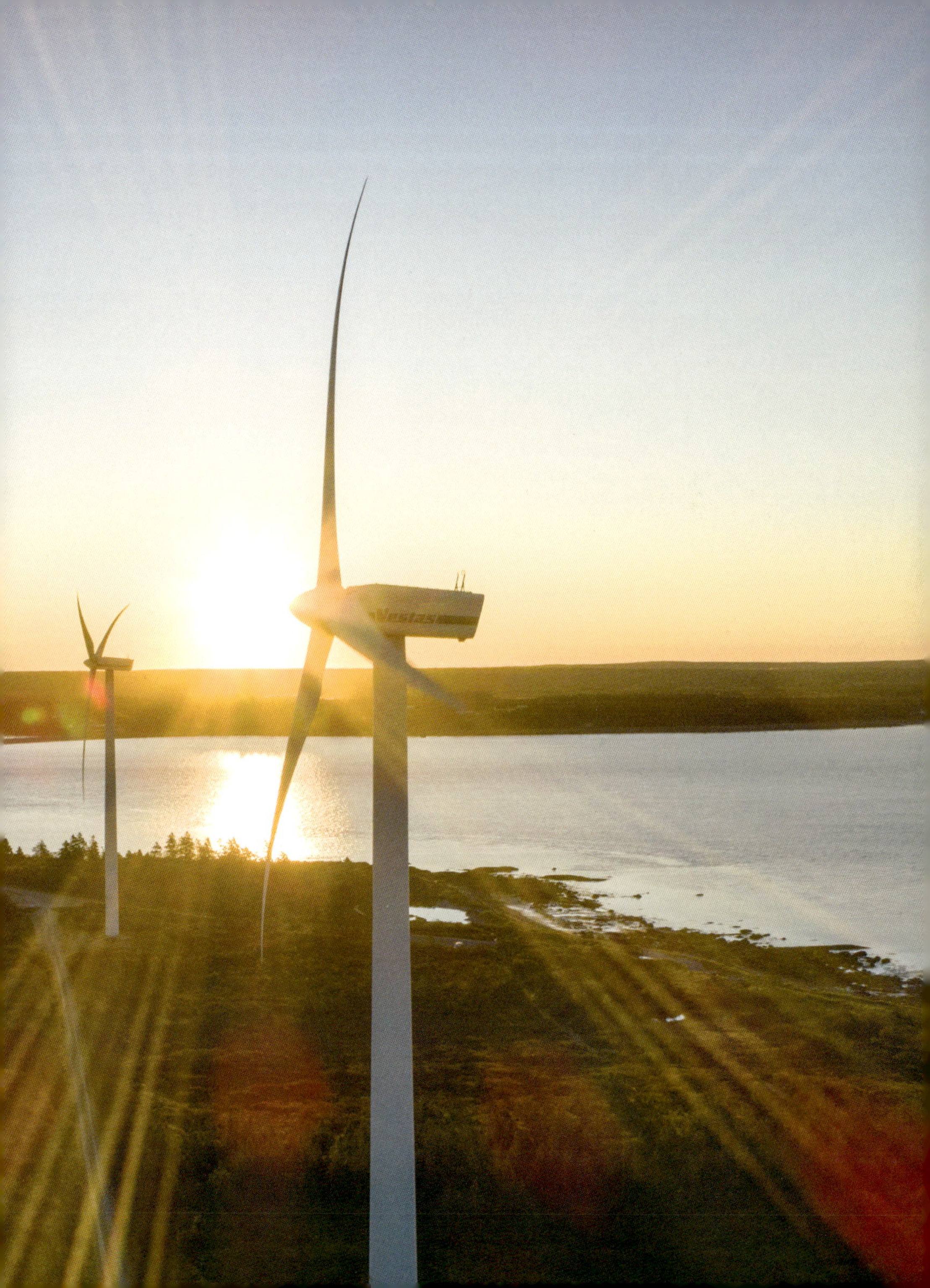
Vestas

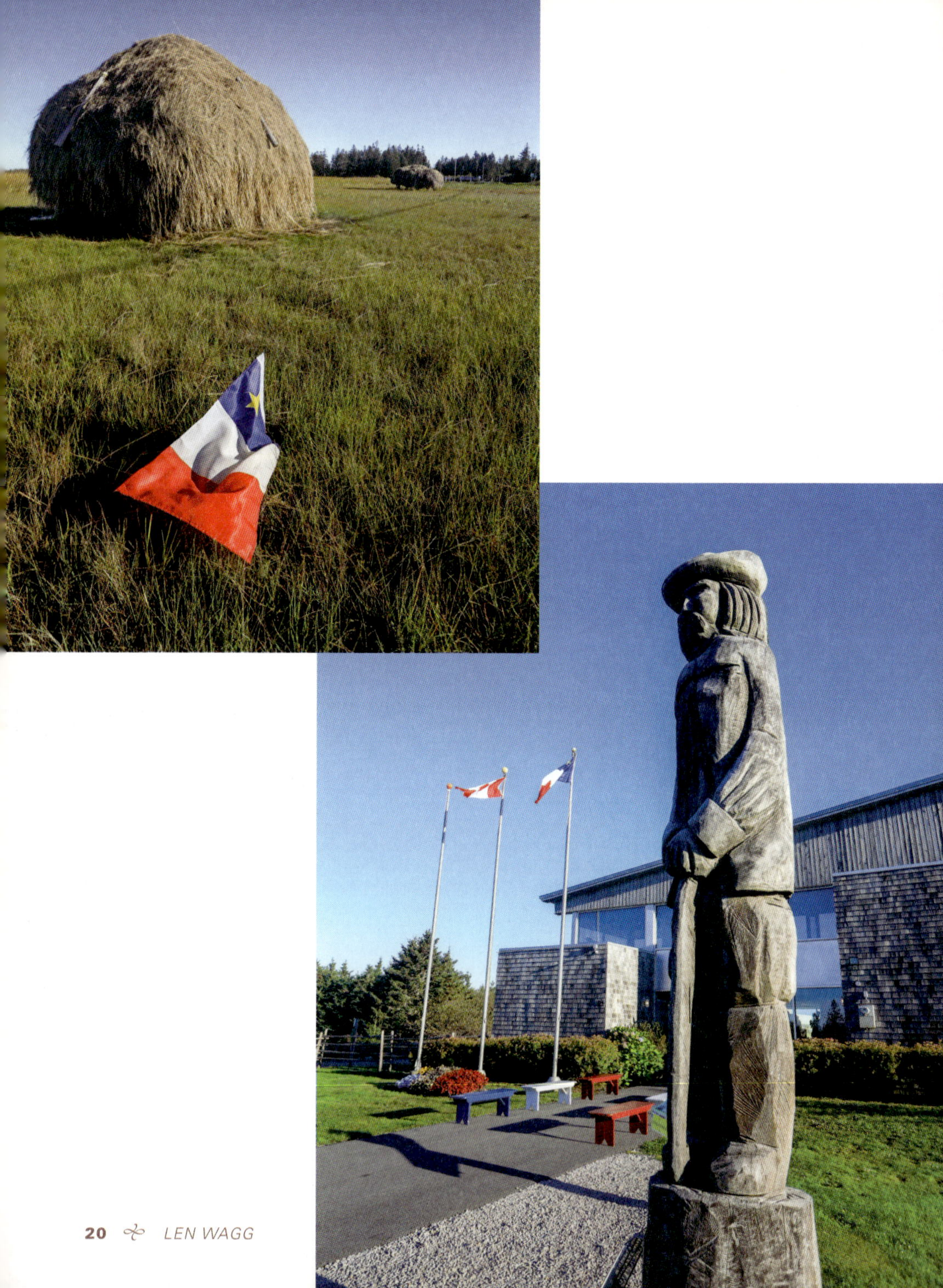

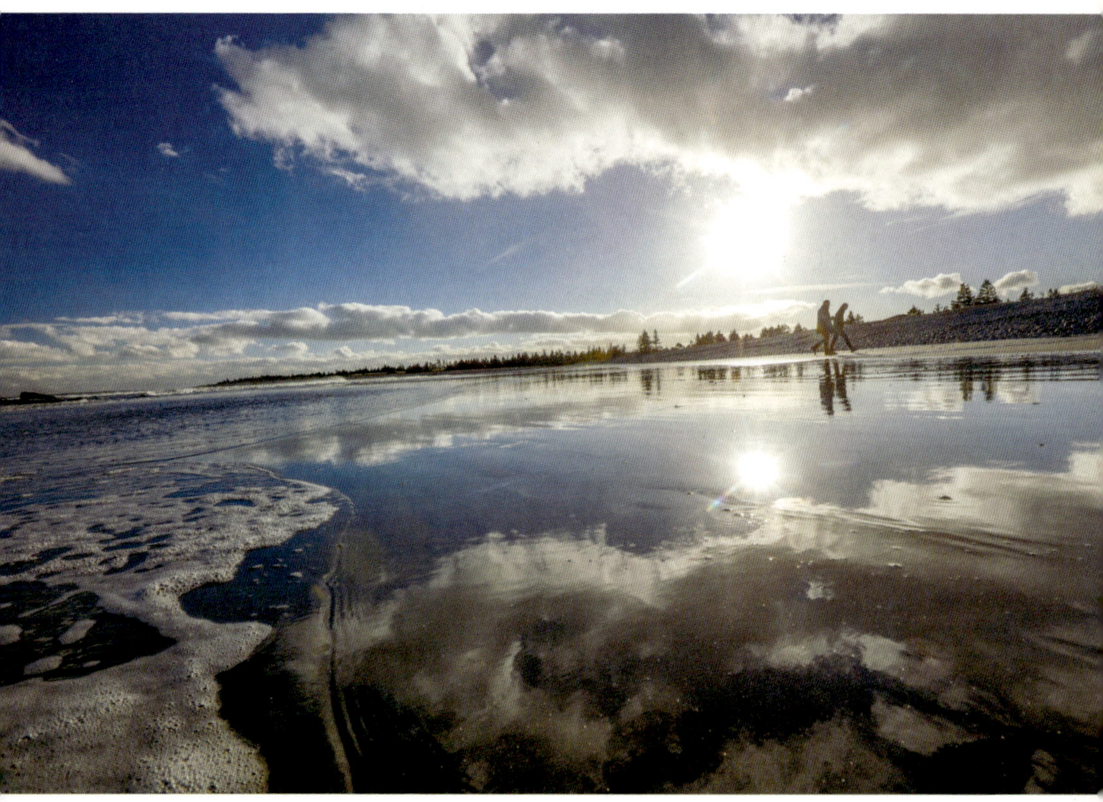

ABOVE ⁓ A couple walks on the mirror-like sand along the beach at White Point.

FACING ABOVE ⁓ Hay, gathered from the coastal lands, is piled high at Sluice Point. The area was once home to thousands of haystacks that were harvested as "salt hay" for the cattle.

FACING BELOW ⁓ A wooden carving of Sir Phillippe Mius d'Entremont, founder of the Acadian colony in Pubnico, stands outside the Historic Acadian Village of Nova Scotia.

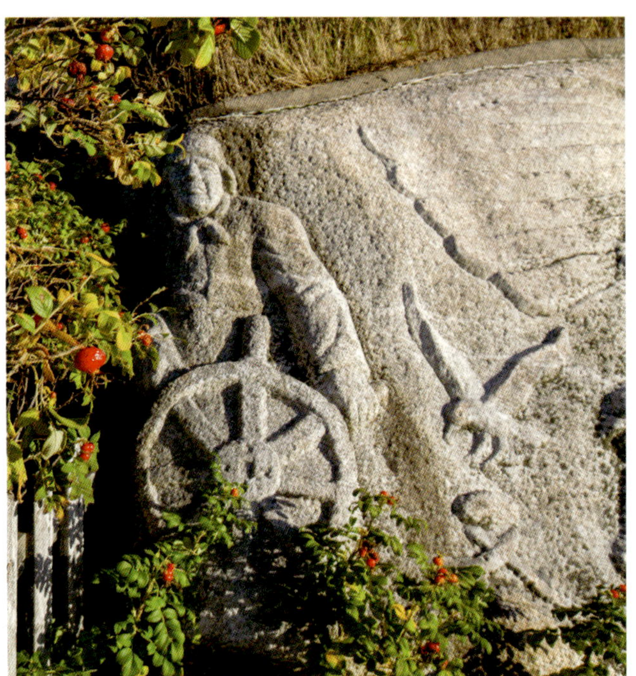

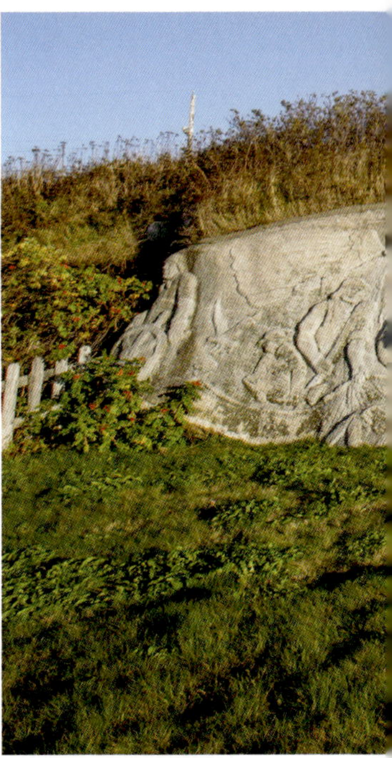

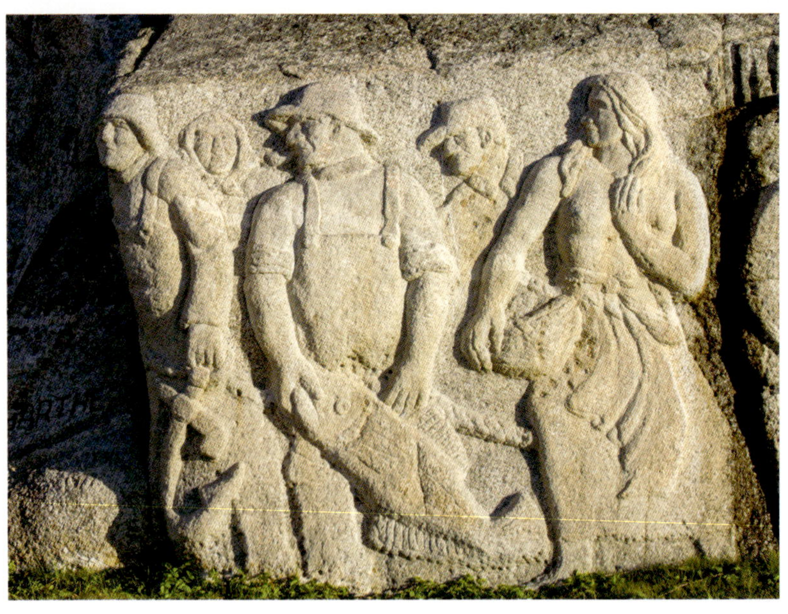

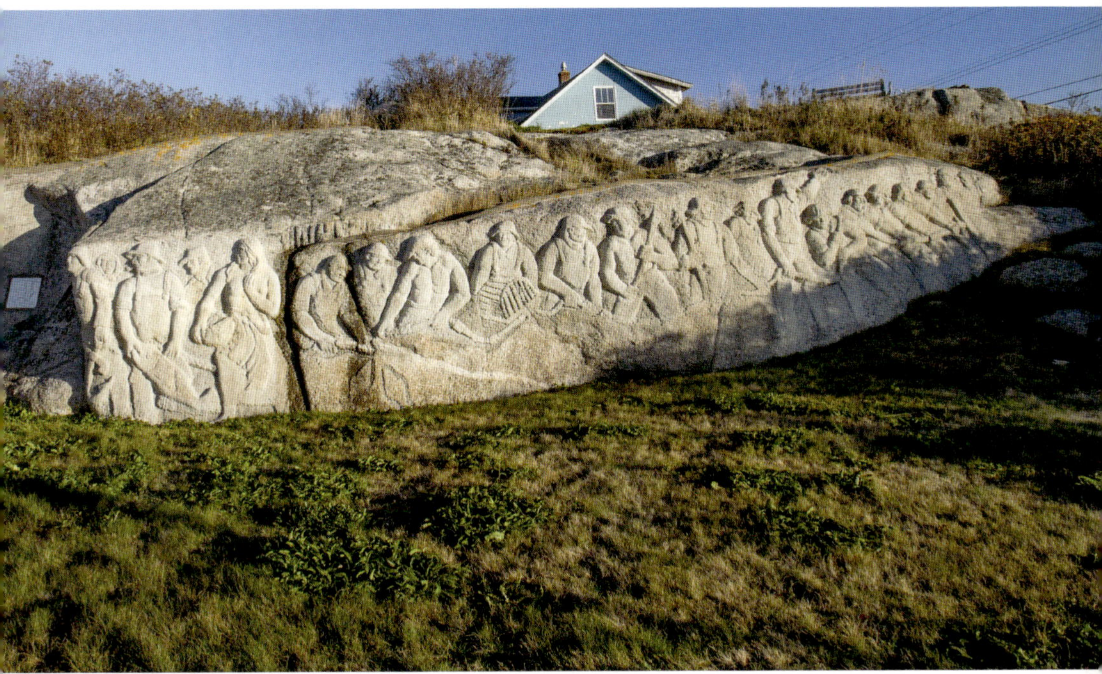

ABOVE AND FACING ⁓ After emigrating to Canada from Finland, celebrated artist William E. deGarthe eventually found himself spending summers in Peggys Cove. In the late 1970s he began a ten-year project to sculpt a "lasting monument to Nova Scotia fishermen" on a thirty-metre granite outcropping behind his Peggys Cove home. In 1976, deGarthe invited friend and former student Rene Barrette to assist him, and they worked on the sculpture together for five years. deGarthe died in 1983, before the monument was finished. His home is now a museum.

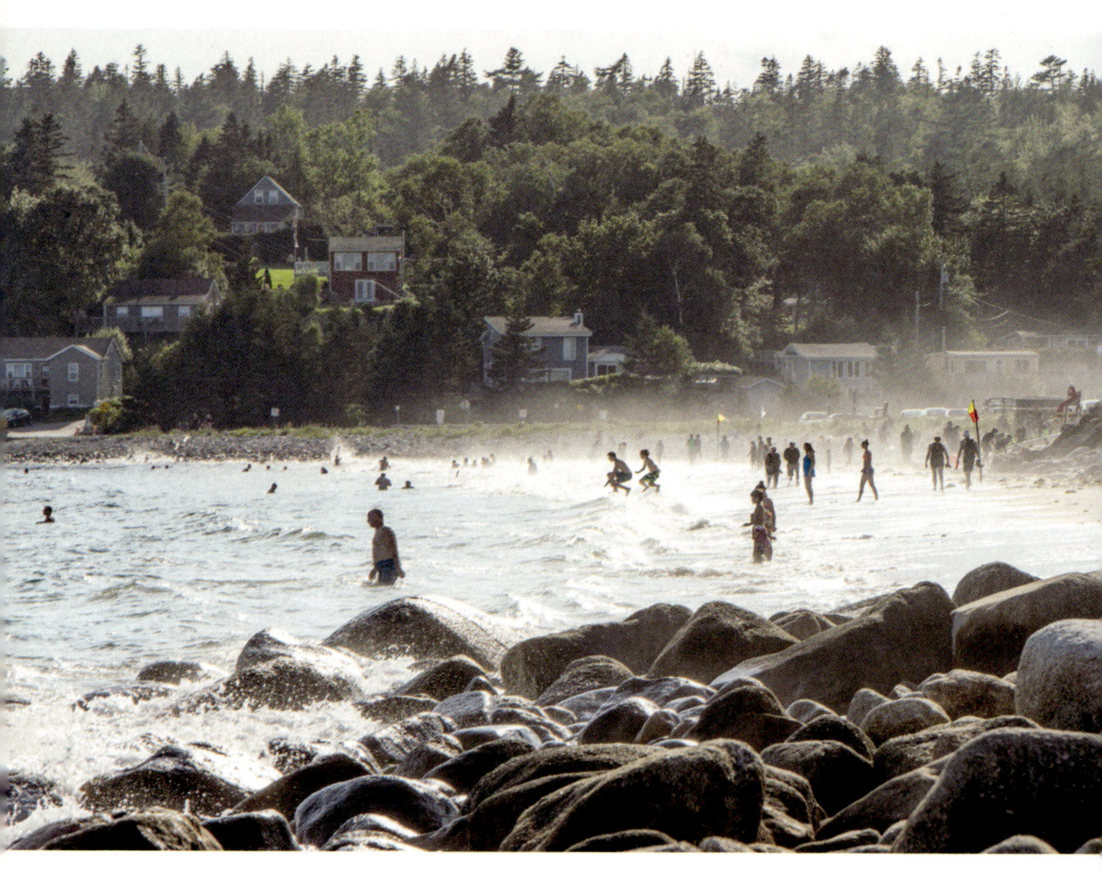

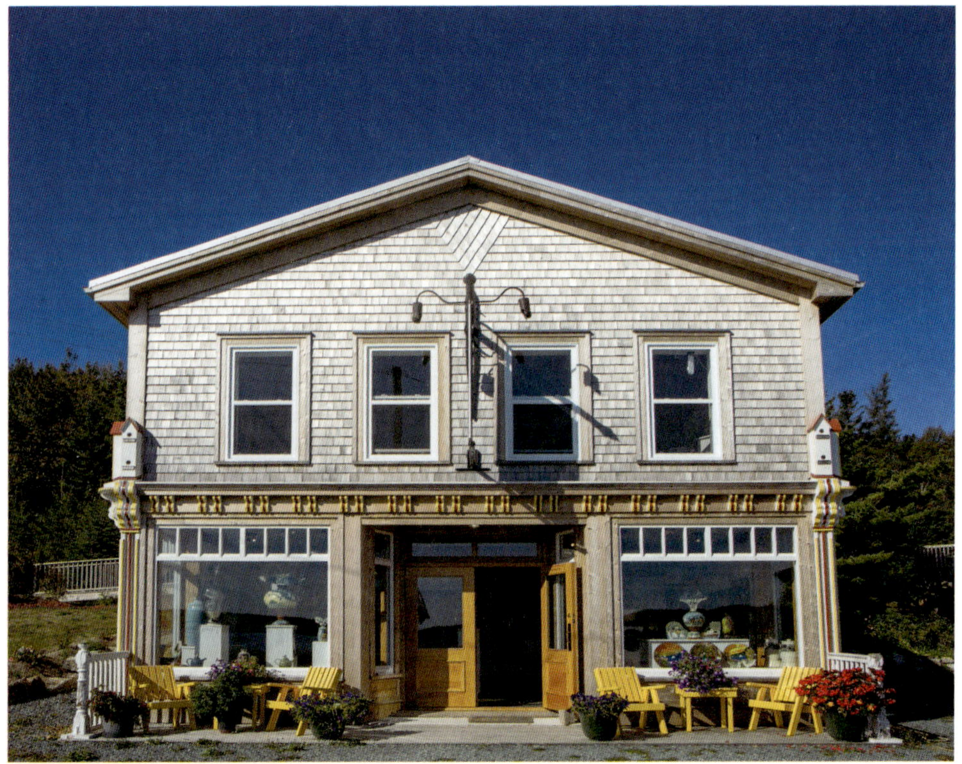

ABOVE ⁓ Highway 331 is lined with shops and artisans' studios, including Westcote Bell Pottery in LaHave.

FACING ⁓ The relatively warm waters at Queensland Beach on St. Margarets Bay make it a popular swimming spot during the summer.

OVERLEAF ⁓ The setting sun and rising tide highlight this perfect Nova Scotia scene at Hunts Landing.

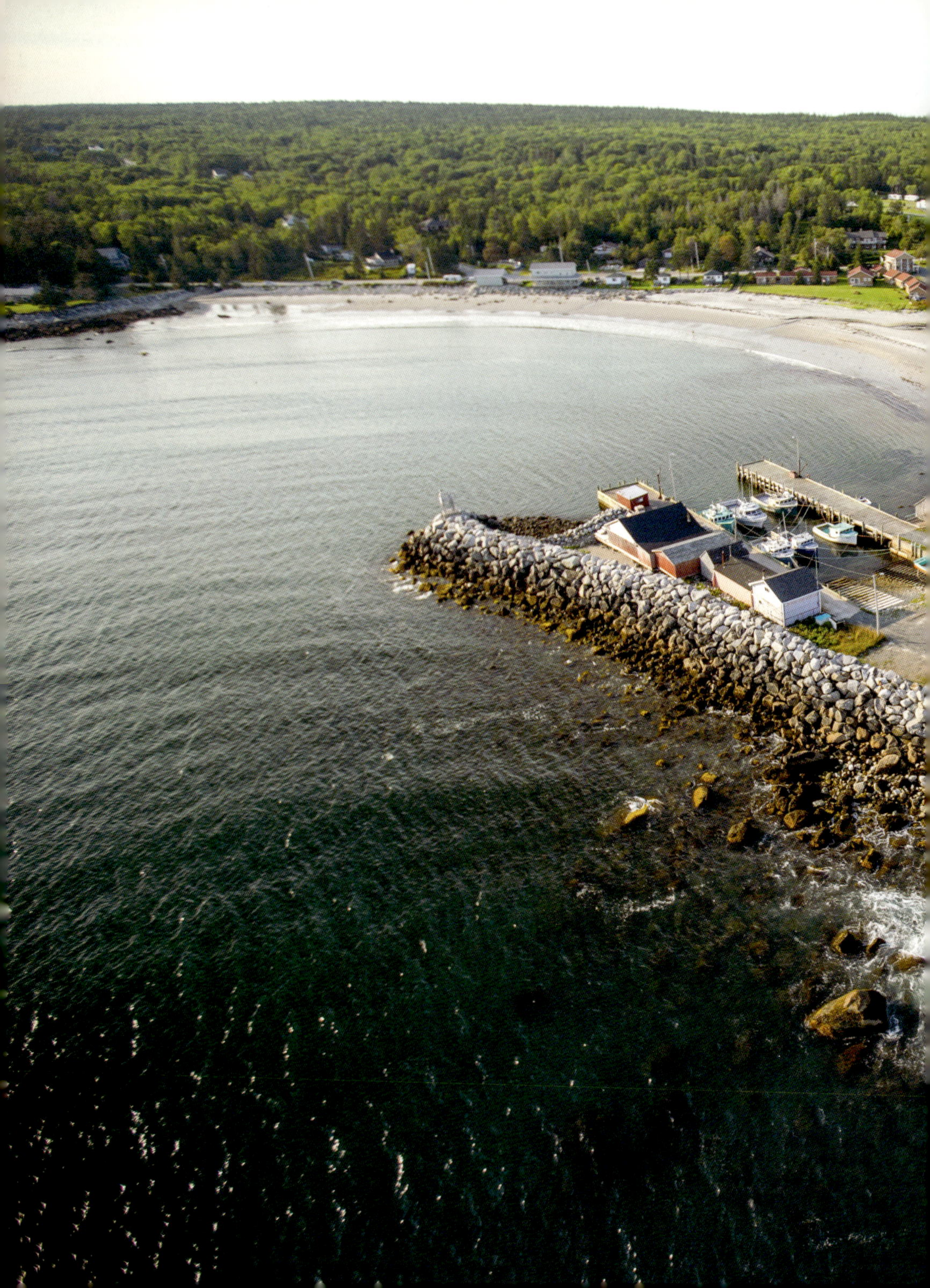

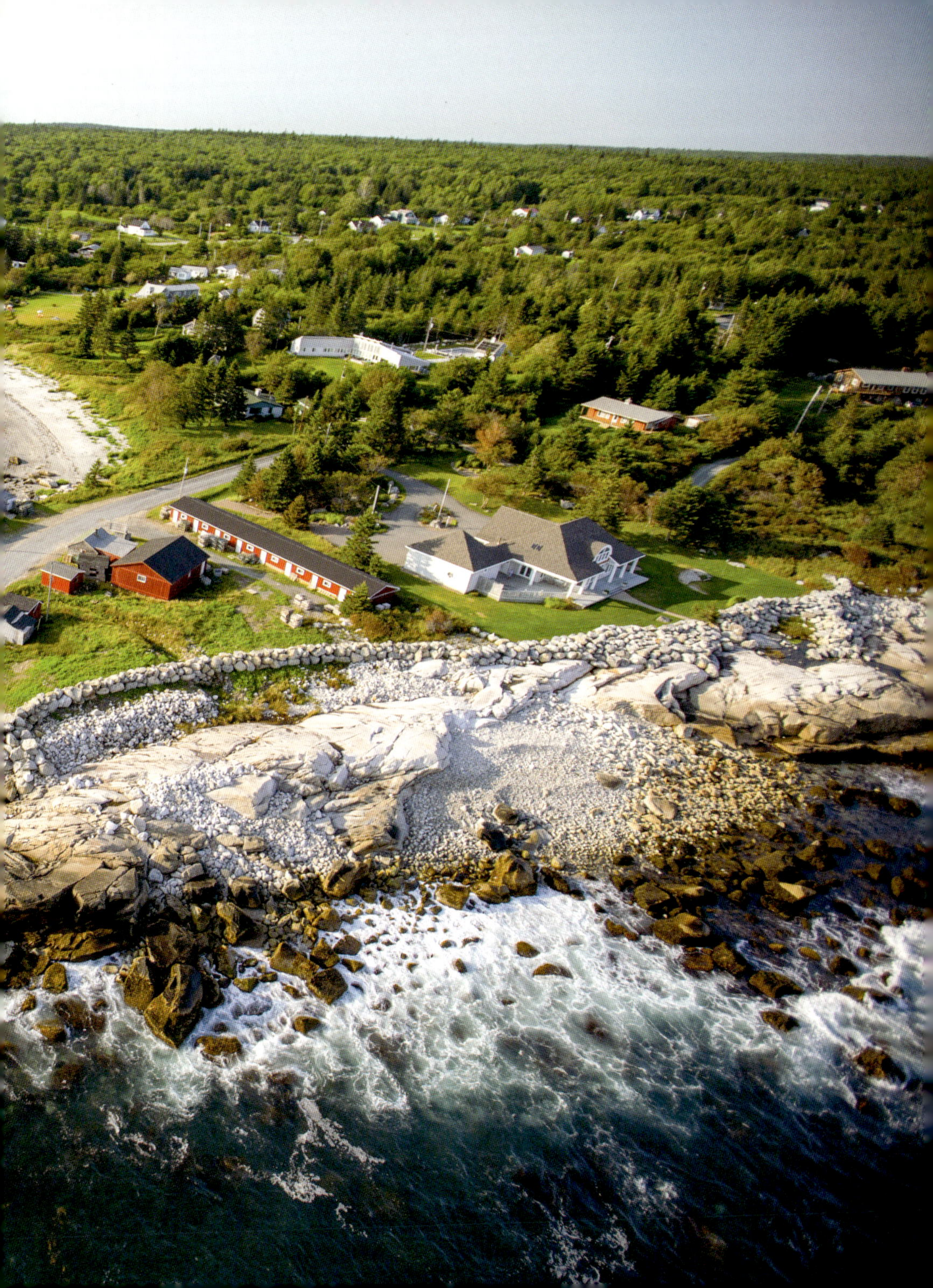

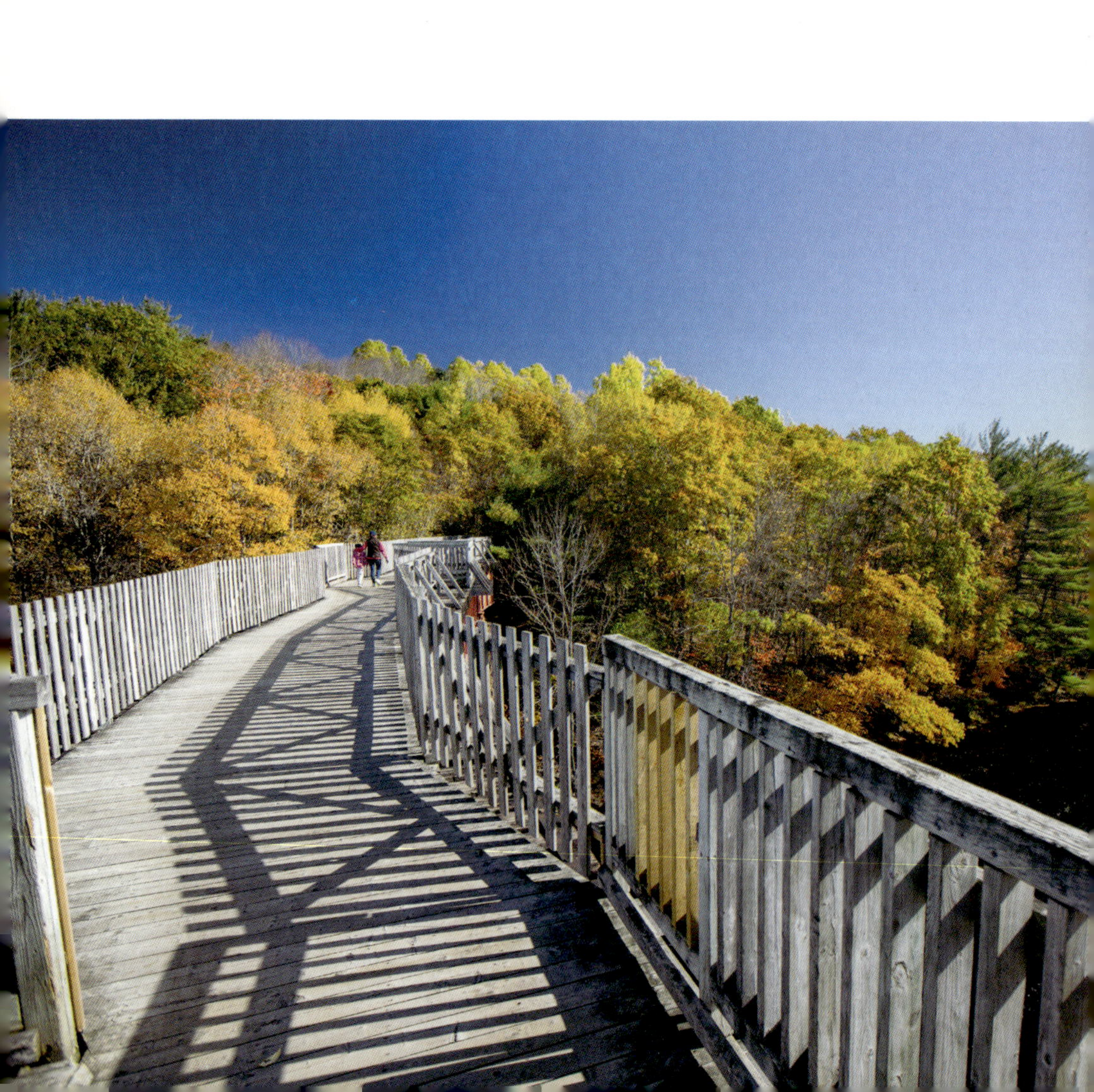

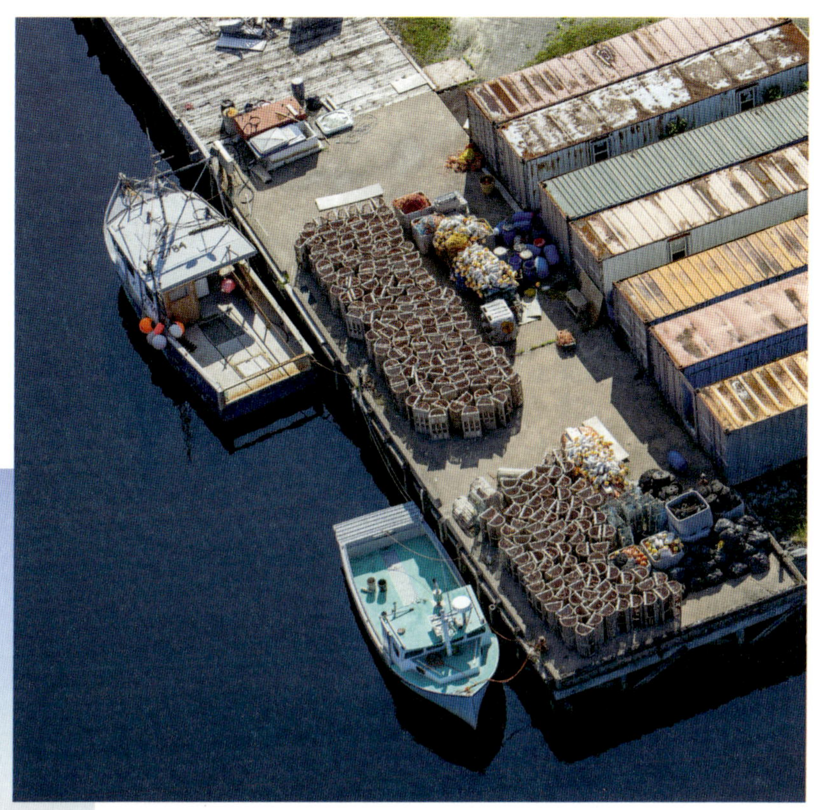

ABOVE ⁓ Fishers organize their lobster traps and buoys along the wharf at Port Mouton before the start of the season.

FACING ⁓ Many of the walking and cycling trails along the South Shore, like this one near Bridgewater, have been built on abandoned rail lines that once stretched from Halifax to Yarmouth.

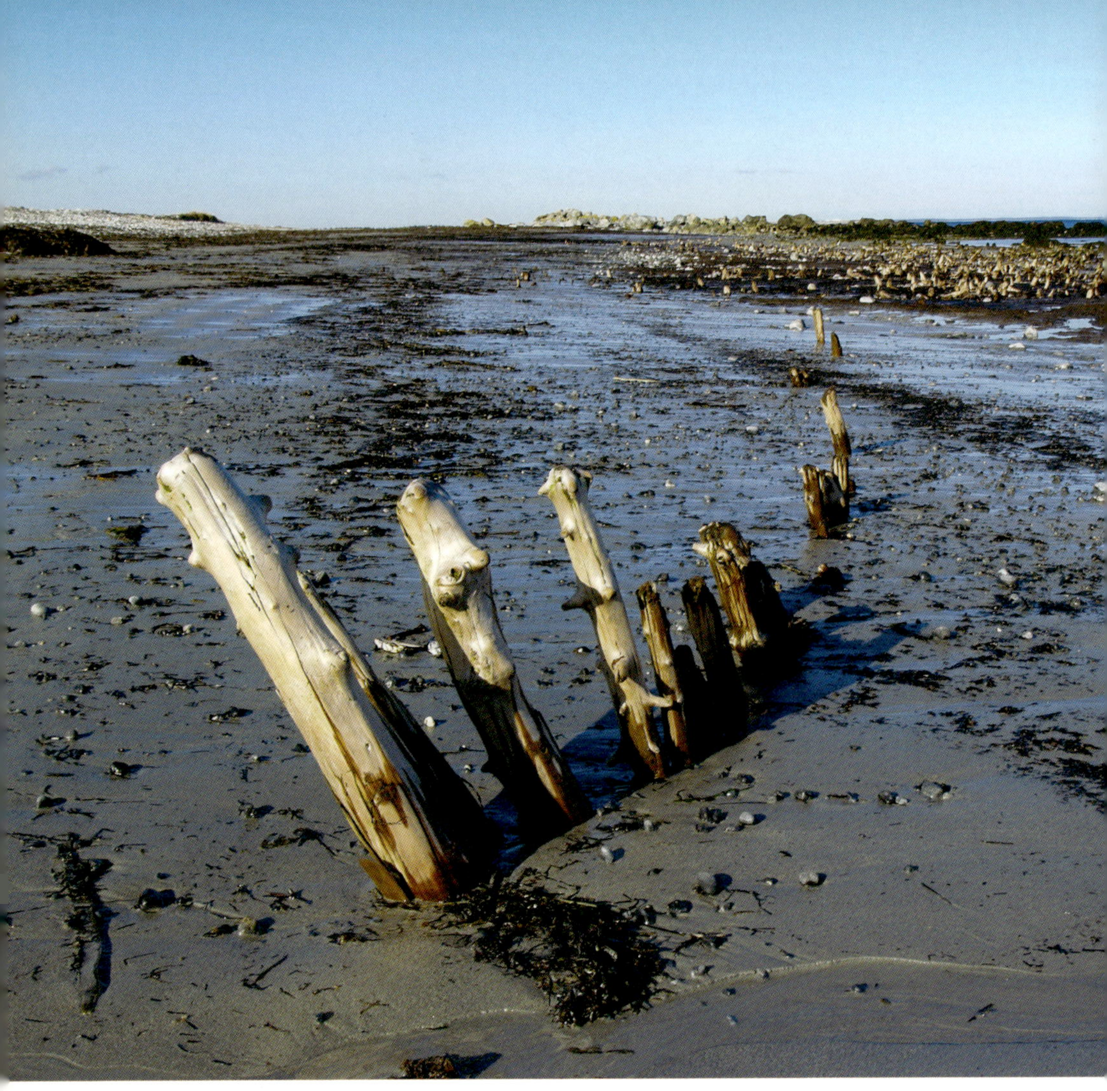

ABOVE ⁓ Low tide at The Hawk on the tip of Cape Sable Island reveals a structure some believe was first built in the 1700s or 1800s. Recent archaeological digs have found more clues to the origin of the wood pilings that are exposed through the sand.

FACING ⁓ The outgoing tide leaves designs in the sand at The Hawk beach. The darker shades in the sand are made by different minerals.

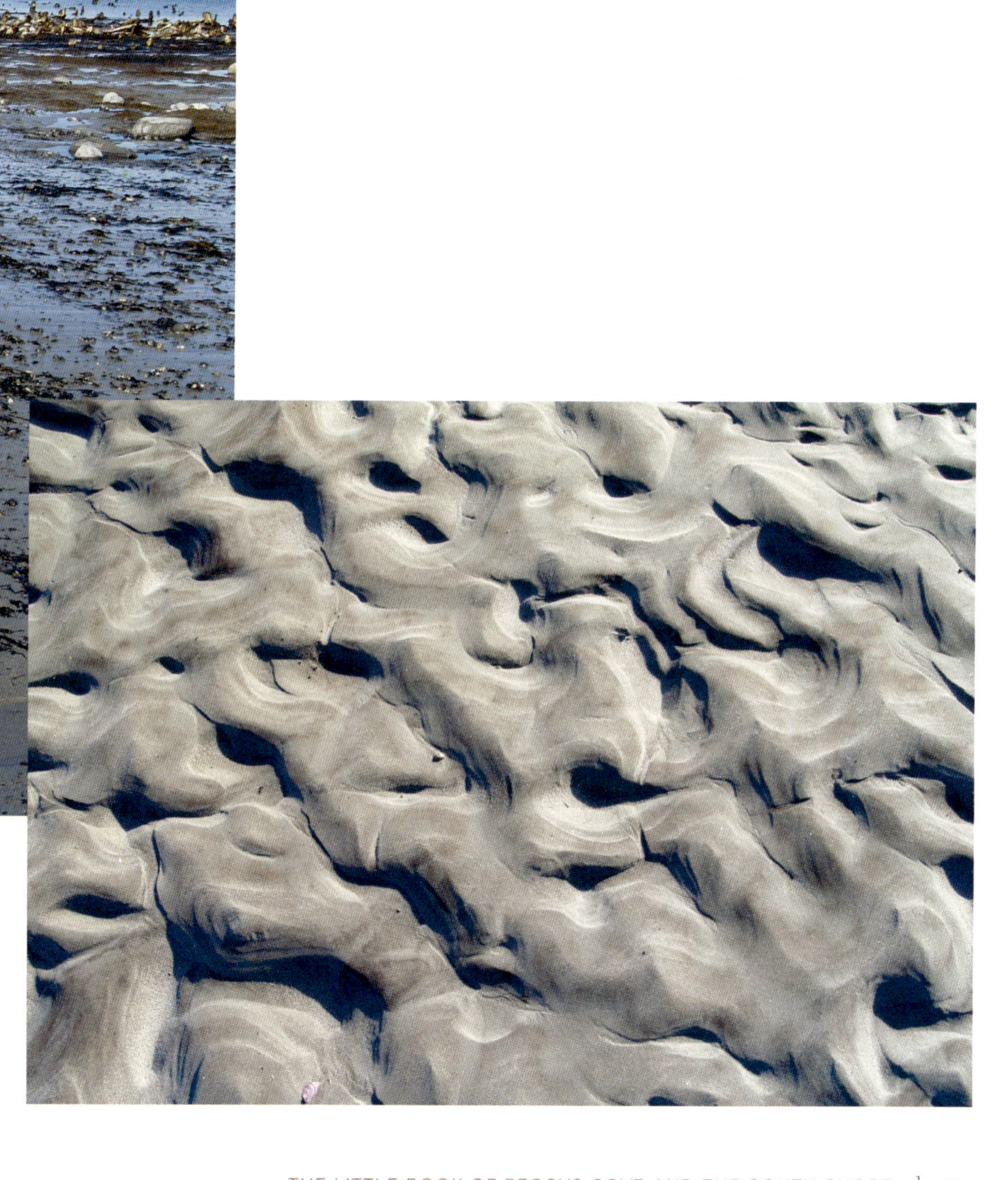

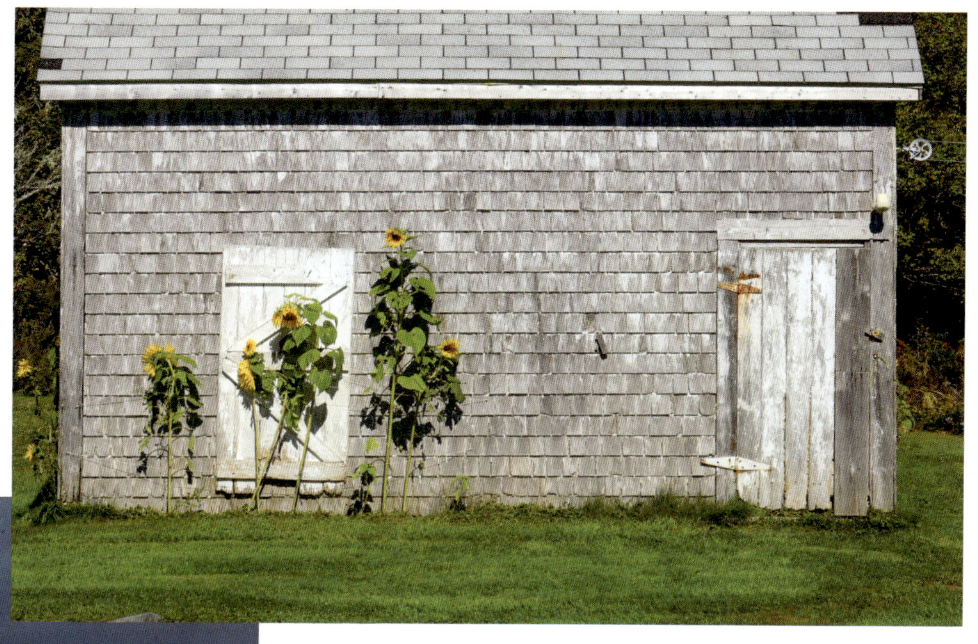

ABOVE ⁓ Sunflowers grow along the south side of a barn near Baccaro.

FACING ⁓ This long nighttime exposure shows a wave crashing against the shore at Cranberry Head. The Peggys Point Lighthouse is visible in the distance.

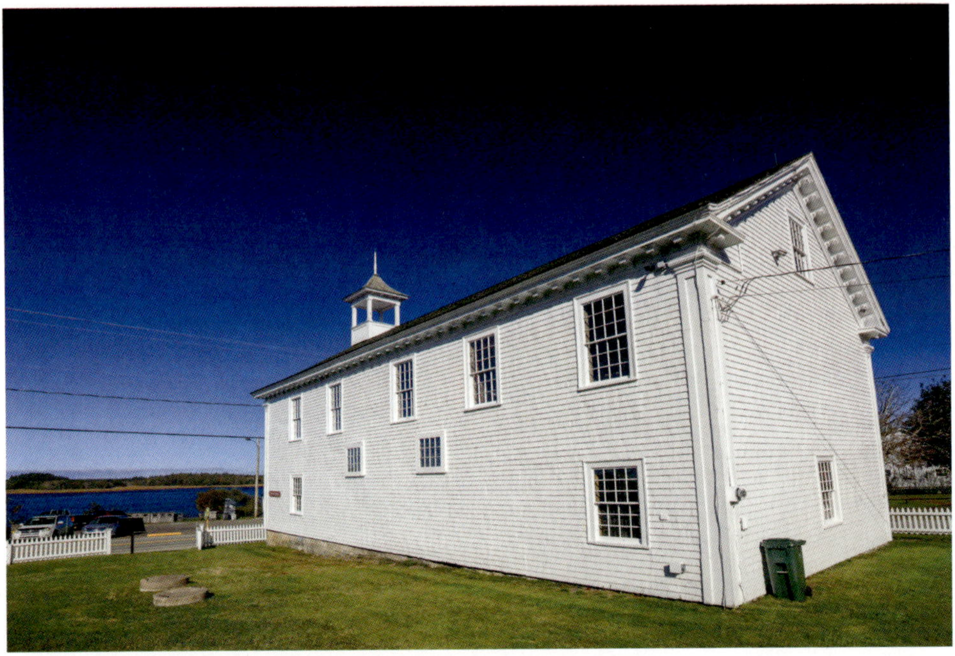

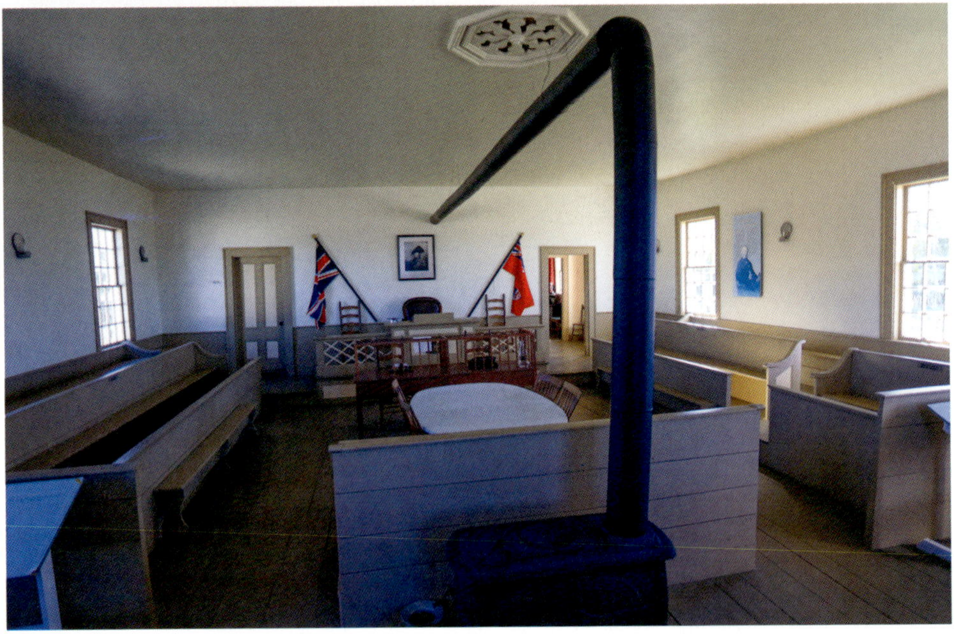

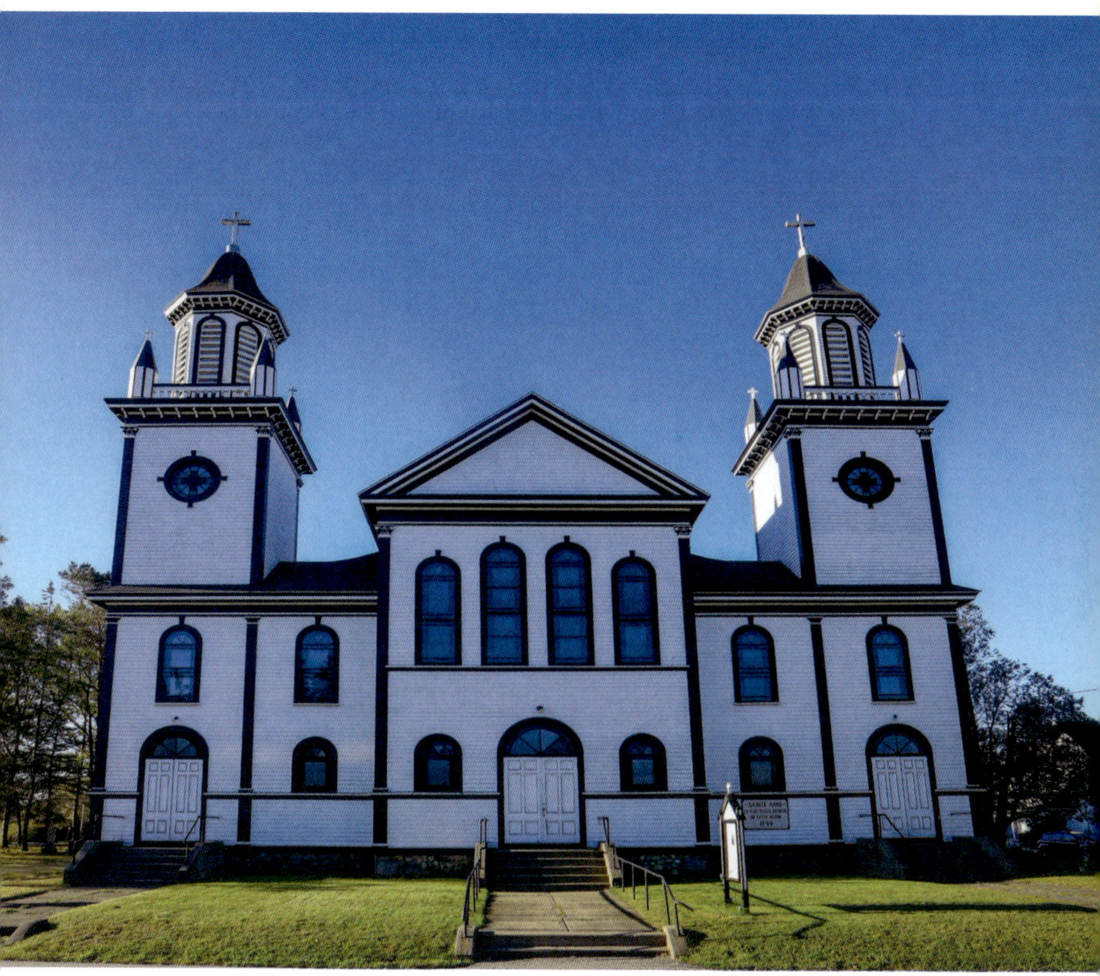

ABOVE ⁓ Sainte Anne's Catholic Church at Ste. Anne du Ruisseau, Yarmouth County, is a Romanesque Revival church that was completed 1901.

FACING ABOVE ⁓ The Argyle Township Court House and Jail in Tusket. The structure, built between 1802 and 1805, is Canada's oldest standing courthouse.

FACING BELOW ⁓ The interior of the Argyle Township Court House and Jail, which now serves as a museum and archives.

OVERLEAF ⁓ A lighthouse on Coffin Island directs fishers to Liverpool and the mouth of the Mersey River.

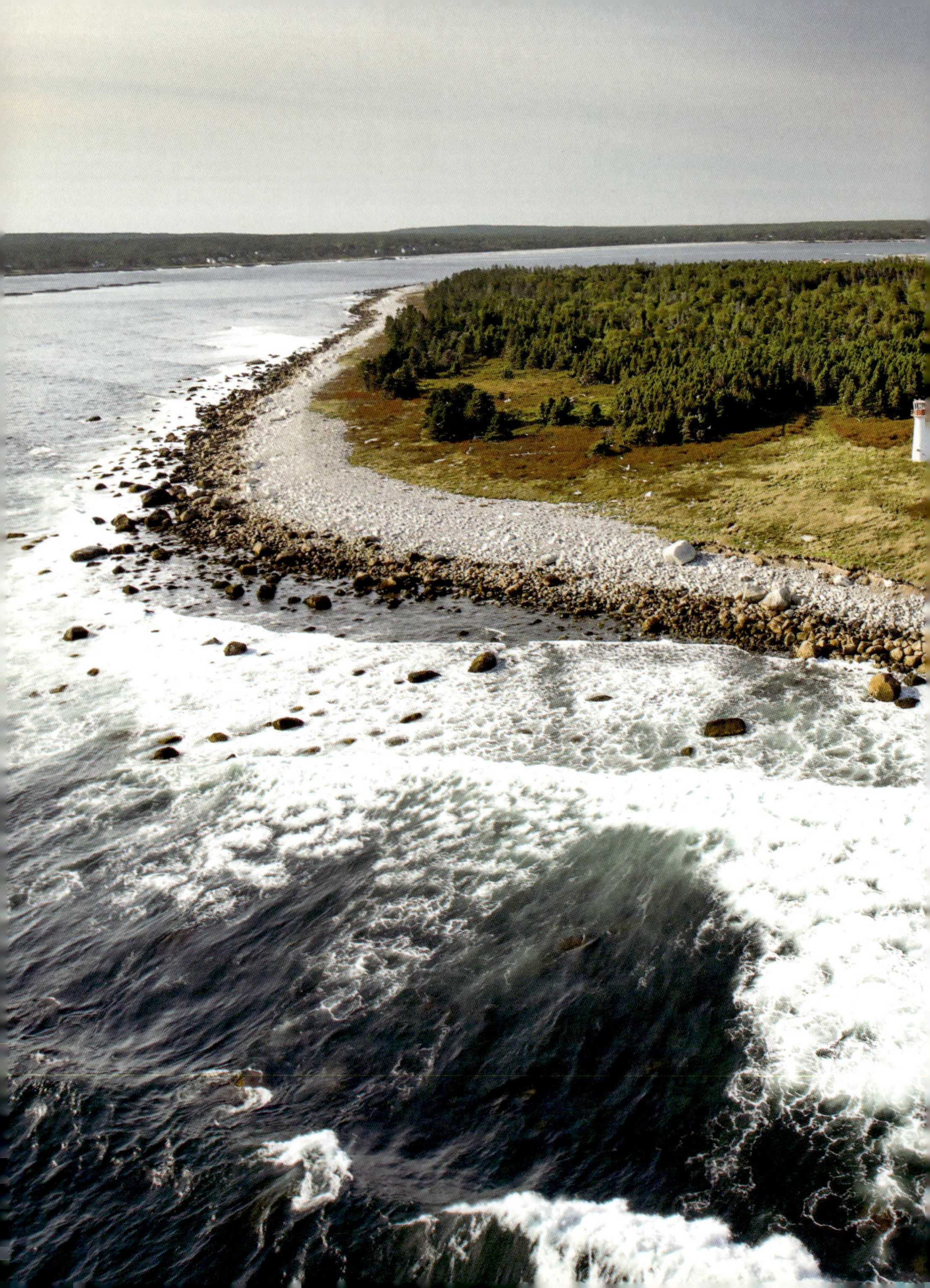

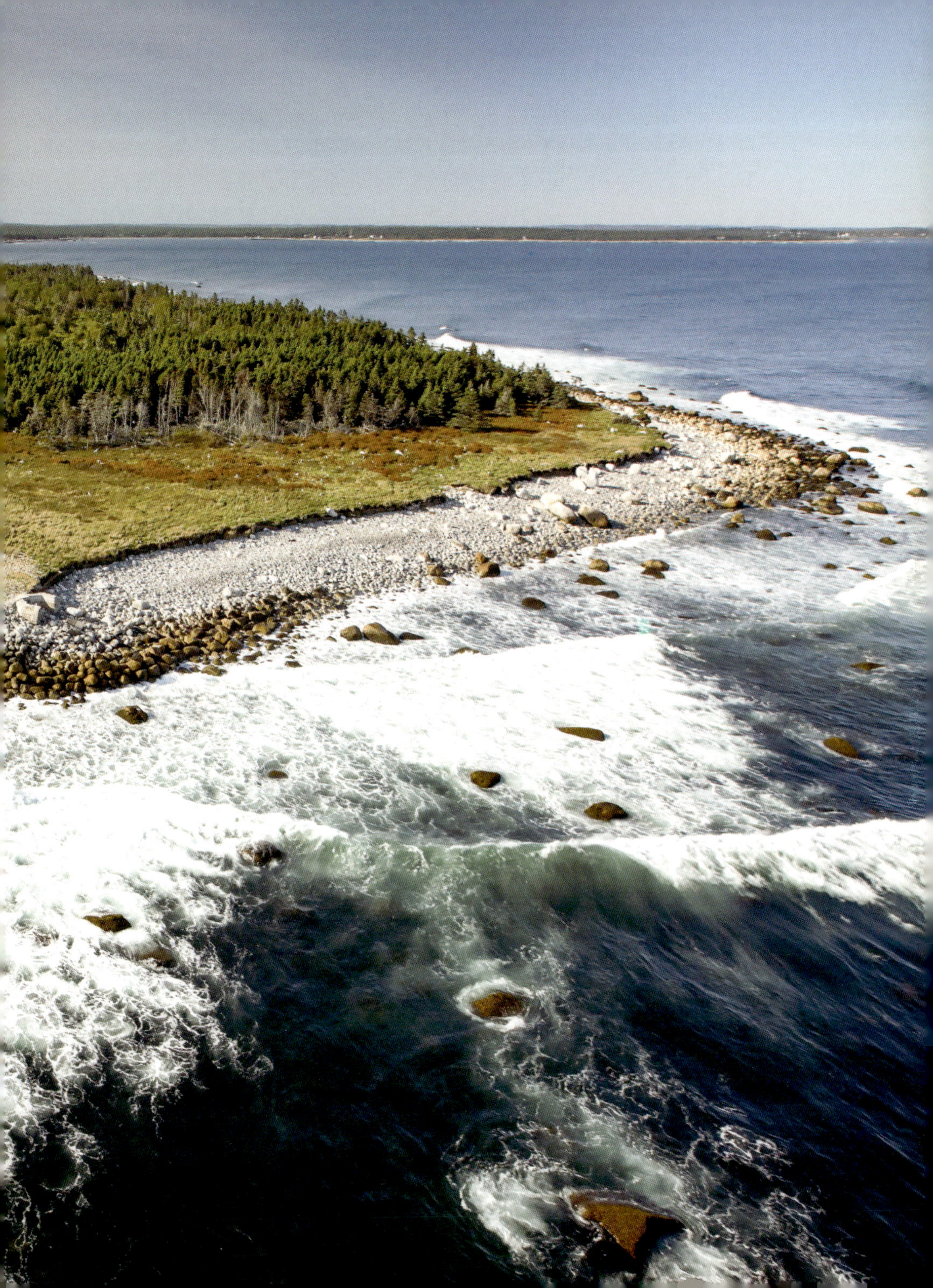

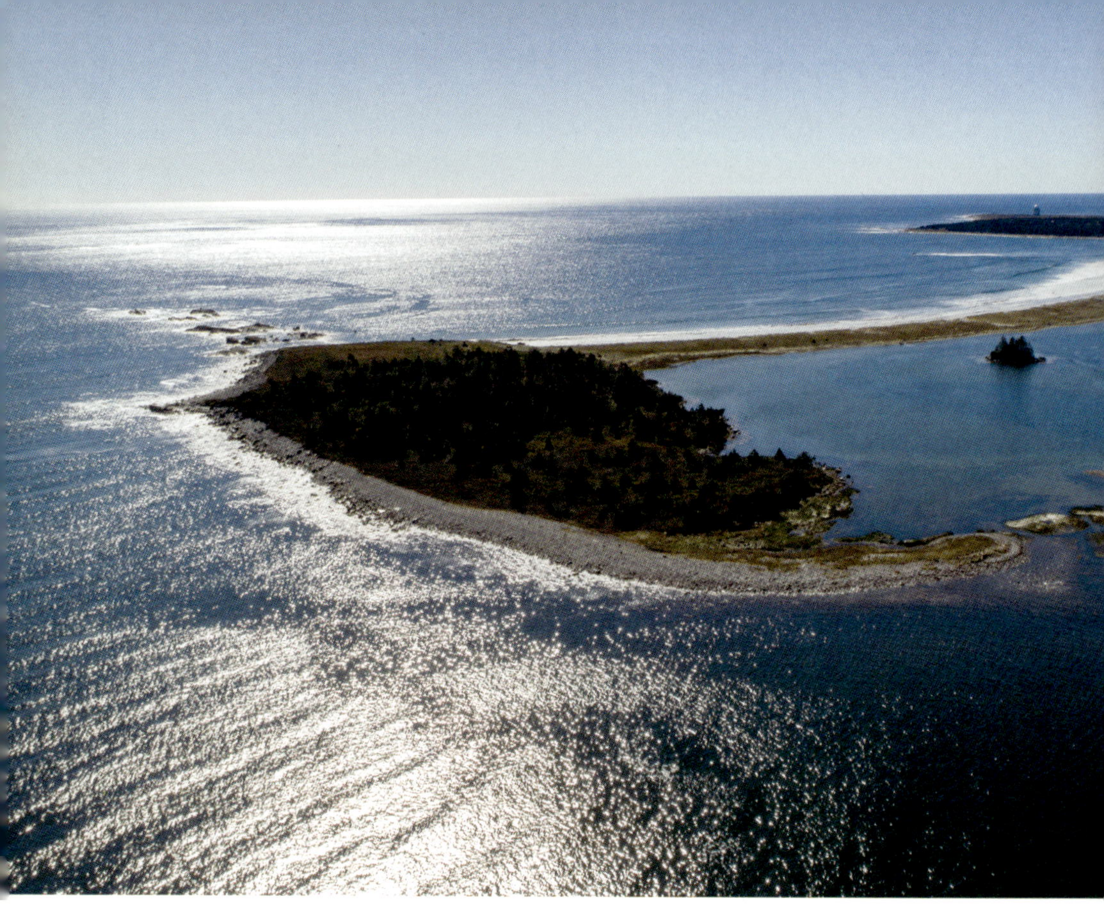

ABOVE ⁓ Waves wash ashore on Crow Neck Island, Baccaro.

FACING ⁓ Three "sisters" at the Dennis Point wharf in Pubnico.

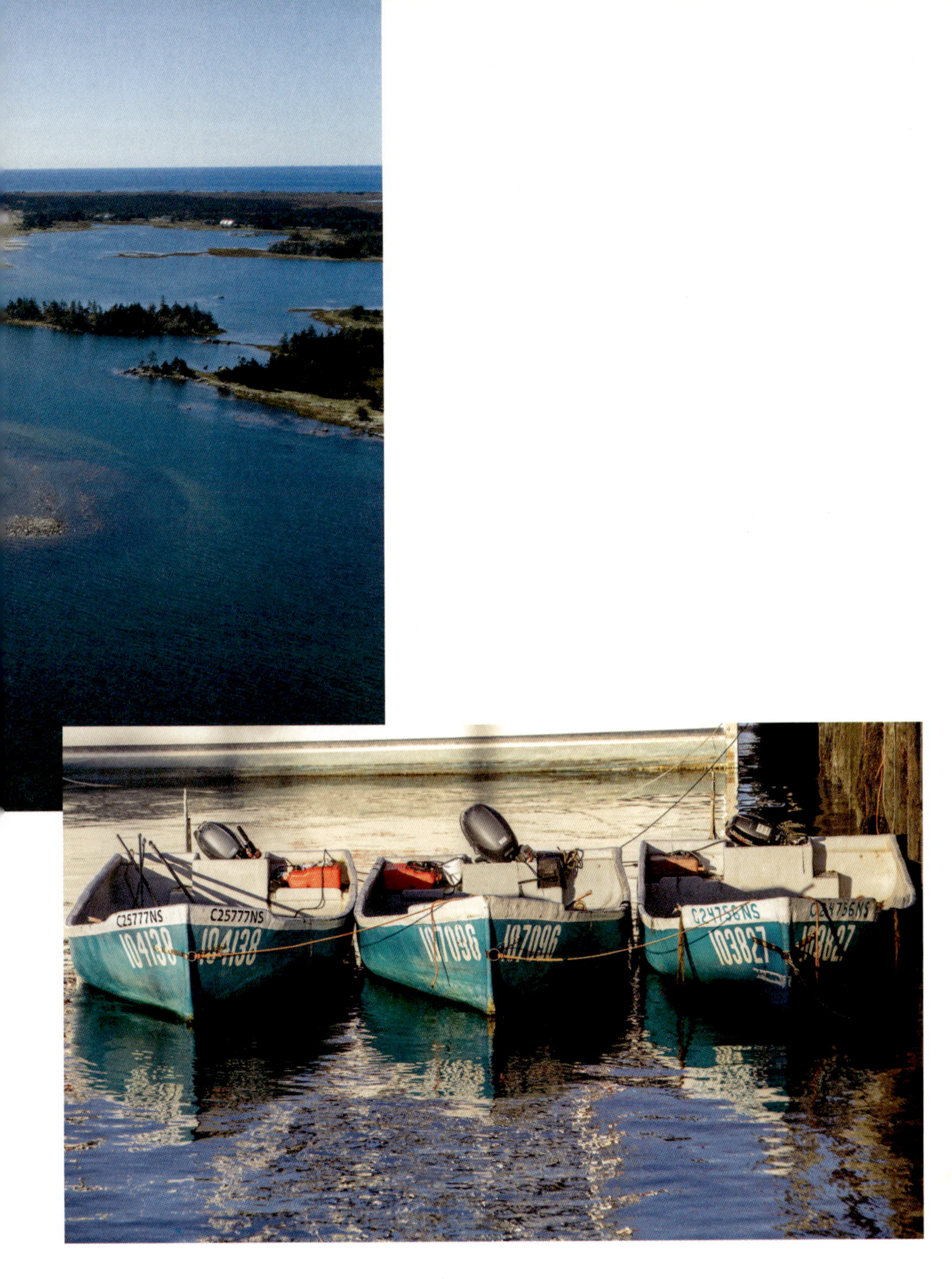
C25777NS
104138
C24756NS
103827

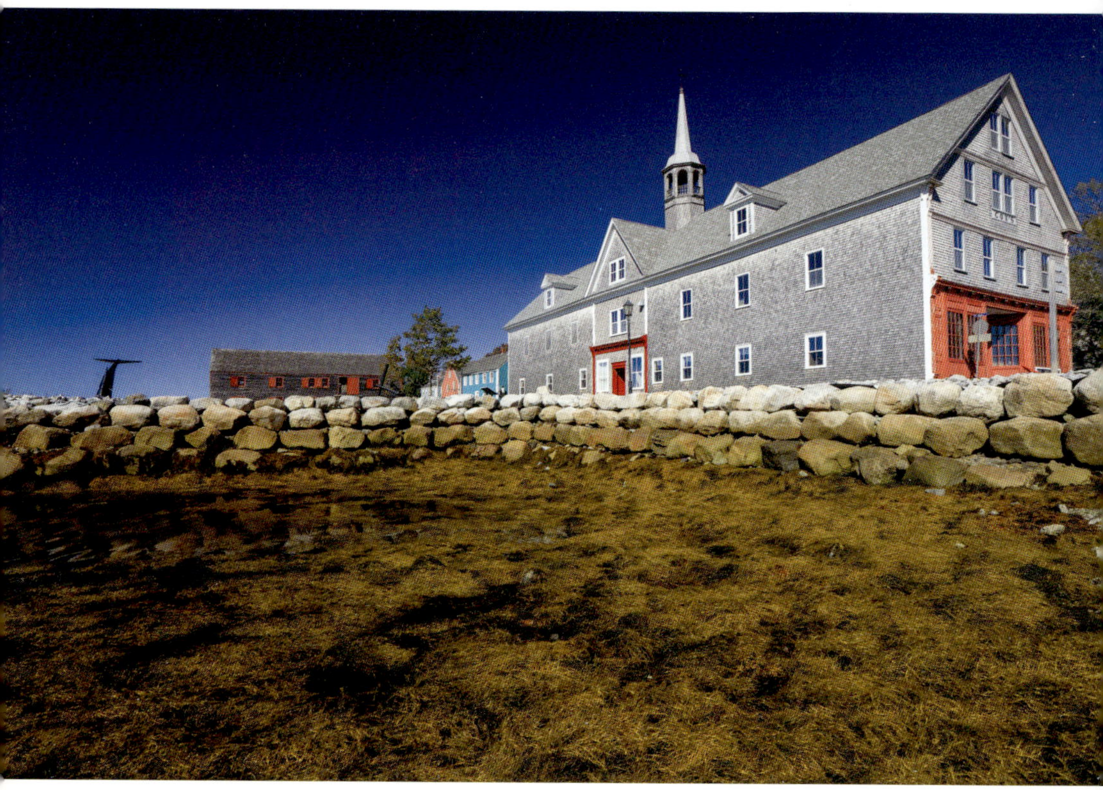

ABOVE ⁓ Cox's Warehouse on Dock street in Shelburne. Built in 1902, the store supplied the shipping, lumbering, fishing, and shipbuilding industries.

FACING ABOVE ⁓ A colourful signpost directs visitors around the Black Loyalist Heritage site in Shelburne.

FACING BELOW ⁓ The community of Birchtown was settled by African Americans loyal to the Crown after the American War of Independence. Today, it is home to the Black Loyalist Heritage Centre, a national historic site.

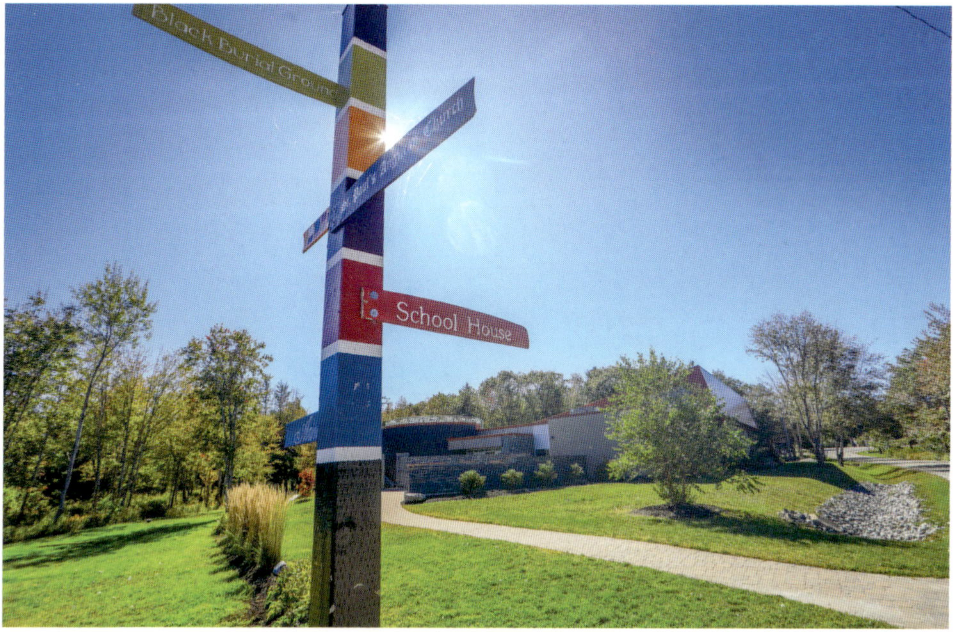
School House

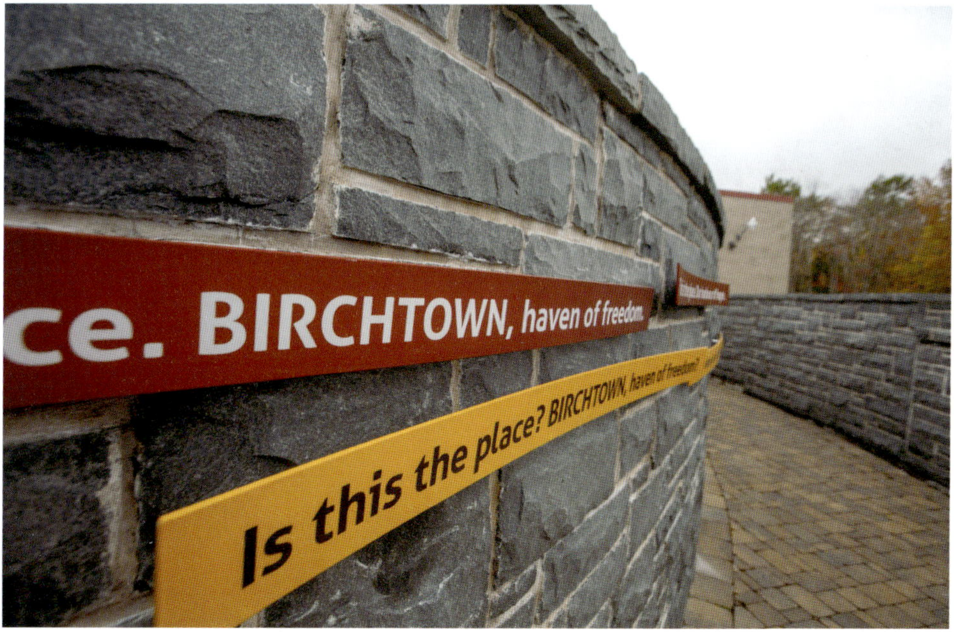
ce. BIRCHTOWN, haven of freedom.
Is this the place? BIRCHTOWN, haven of freedom

BELOW ⁓ A fresh coat of paint on the barn doors at Baccaro.

FACING ⁓ The Locke Family Streetscape in Lockeport is Nova Scotia's first Provincially Registered Streetscape. It features original Colonial, Victorian, and Georgian homes.

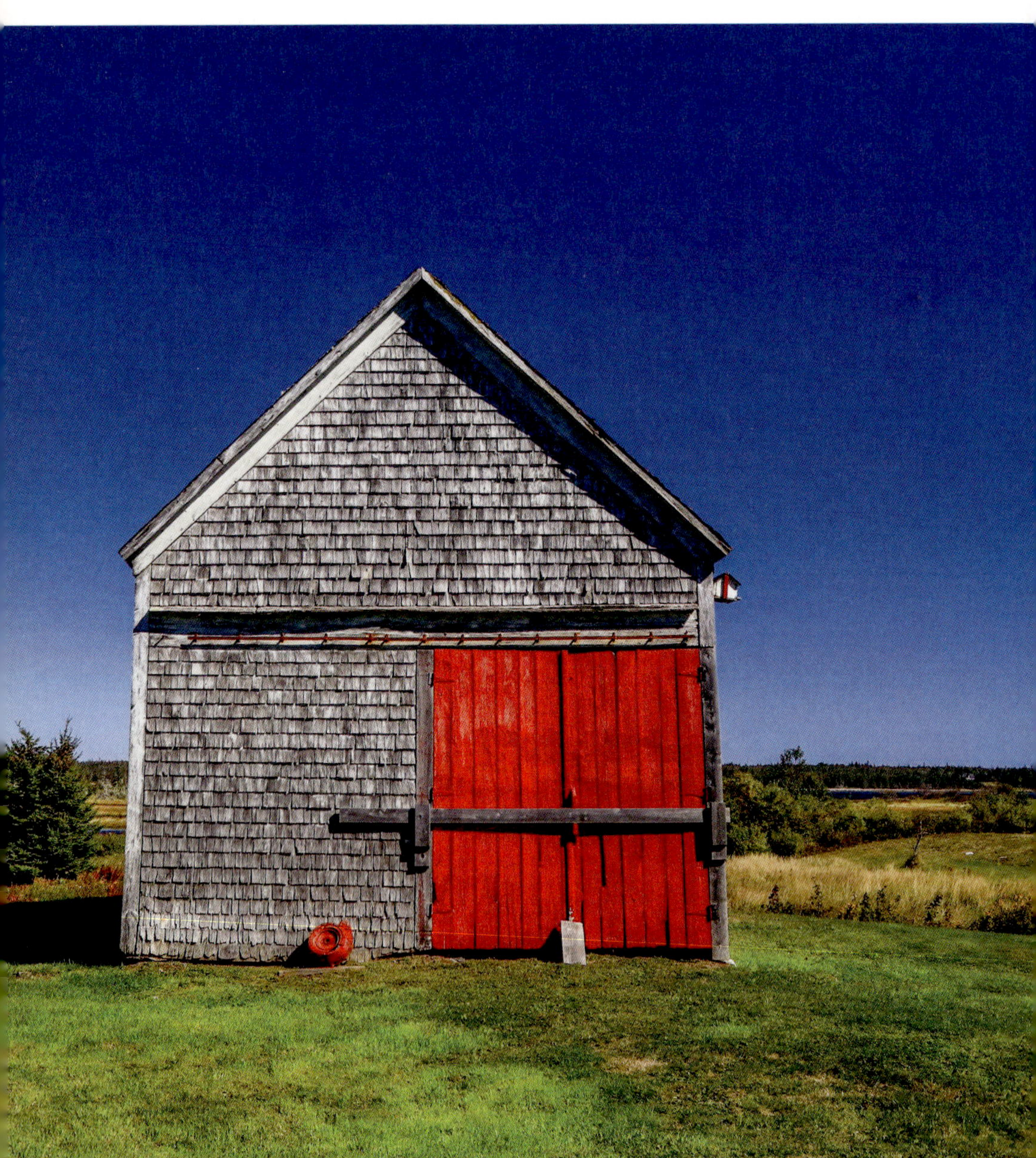

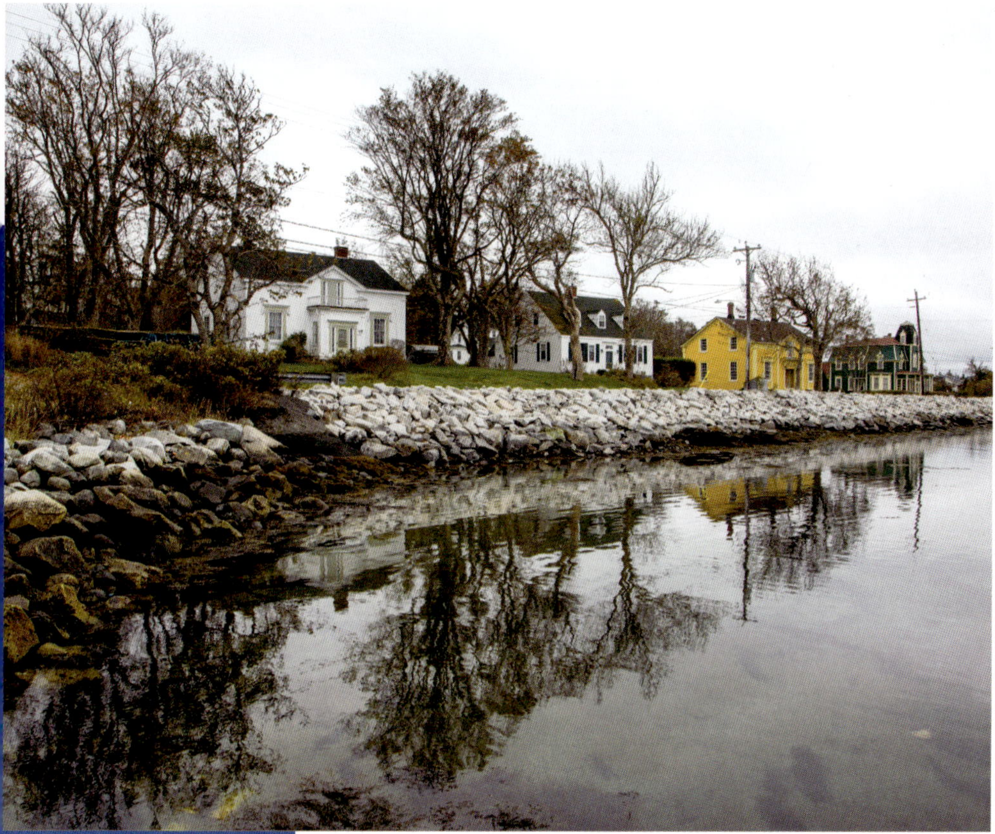

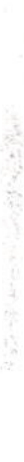

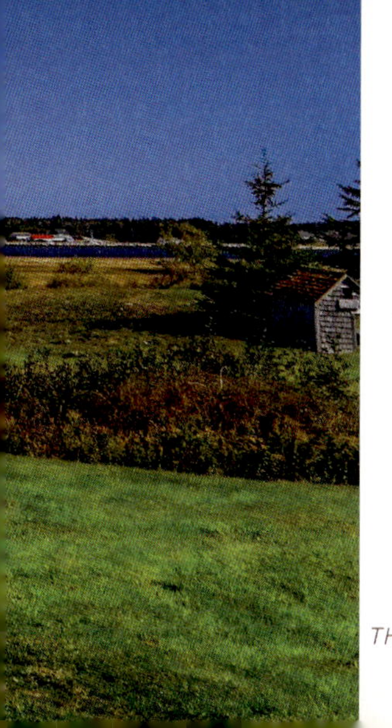

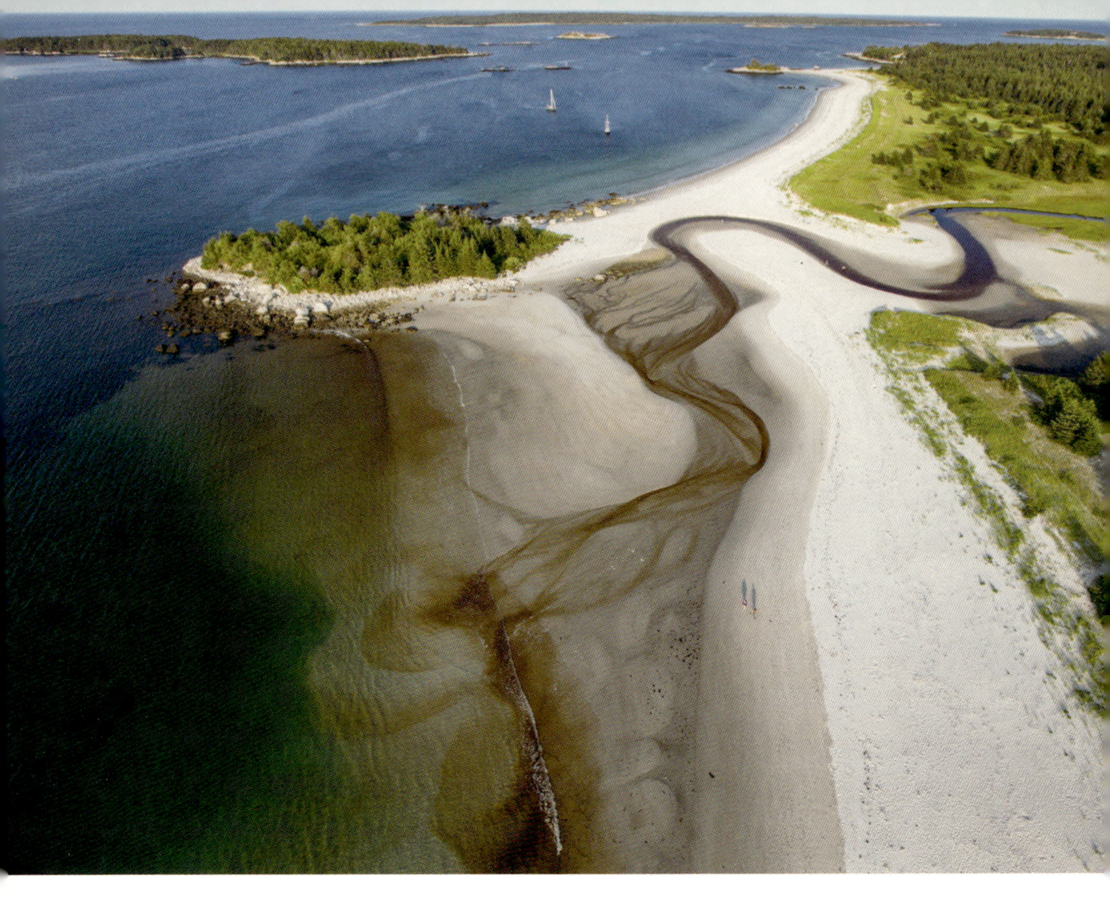

BELOW ⁓ *Bluenose II*, captained by Phil Watson, leaves its home port of Lunenburg, followed closely by the tall ship *Picton Castle*.

FACING ⁓ A couple strolls by the water on Carters Beach at Port Mouton.

OVERLEAF ⁓ Kelp is piled in the shape of a heart near the outgoing tide at Hirtles Beach near Kingsburg.

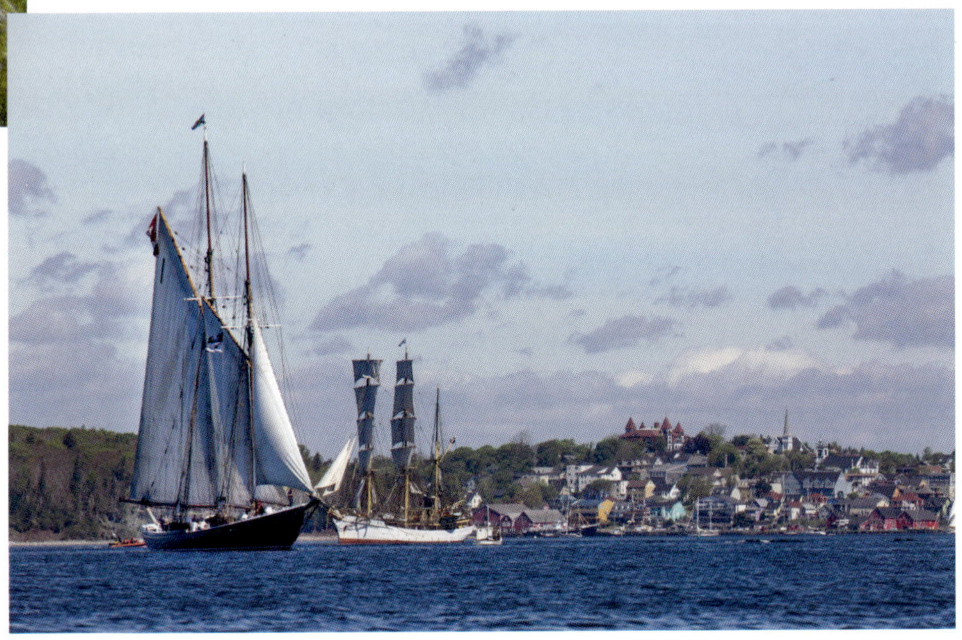

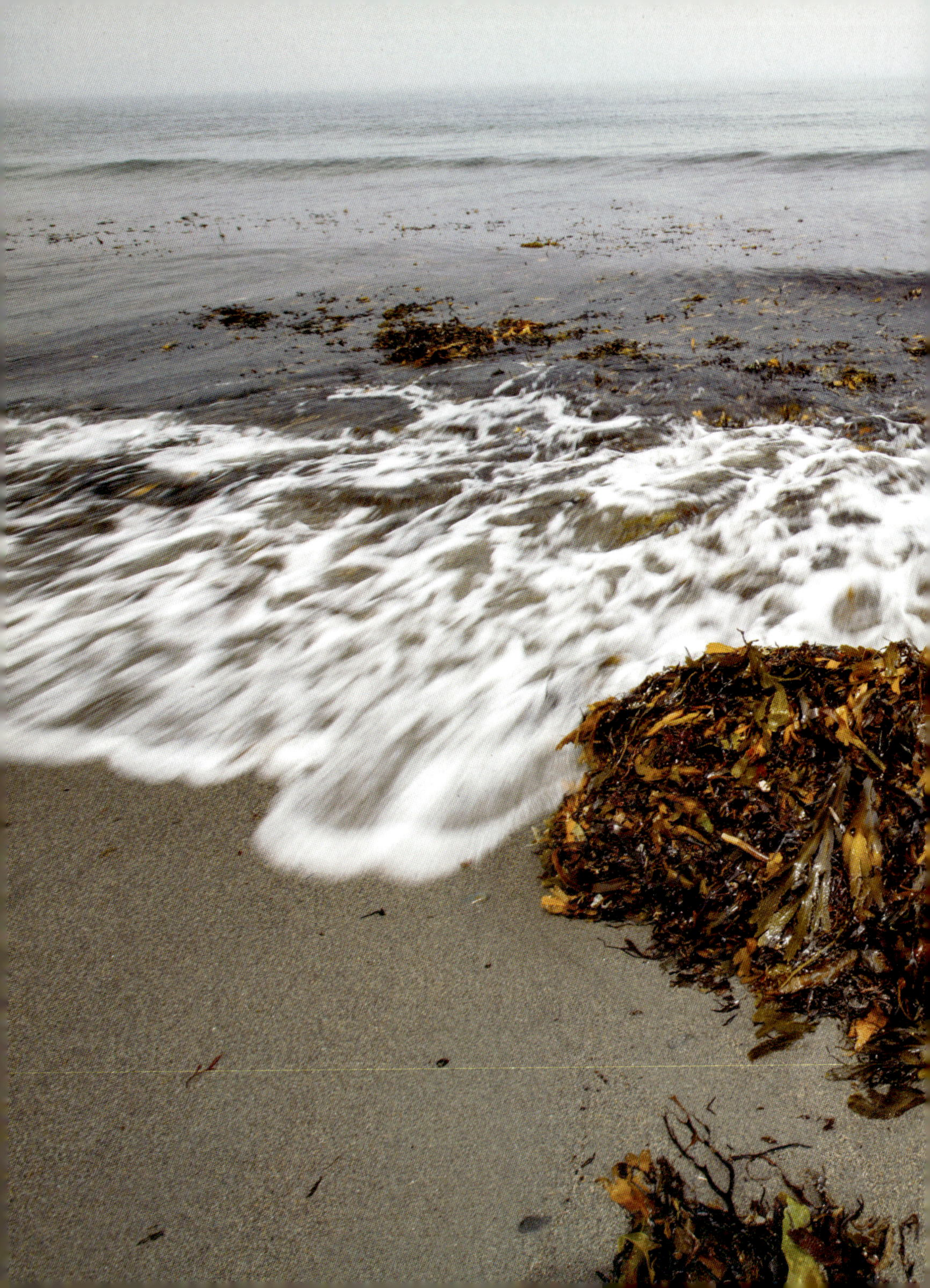

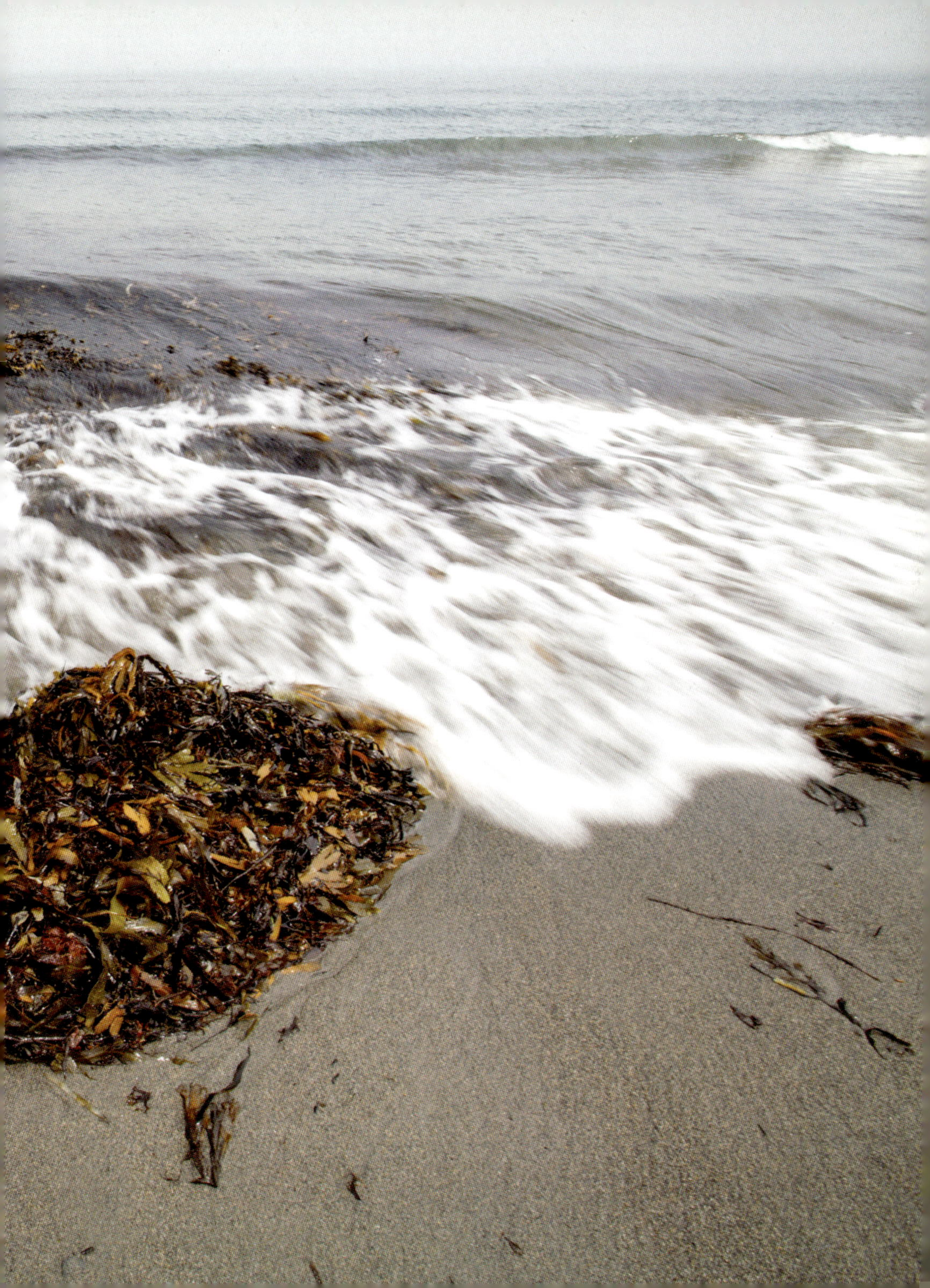

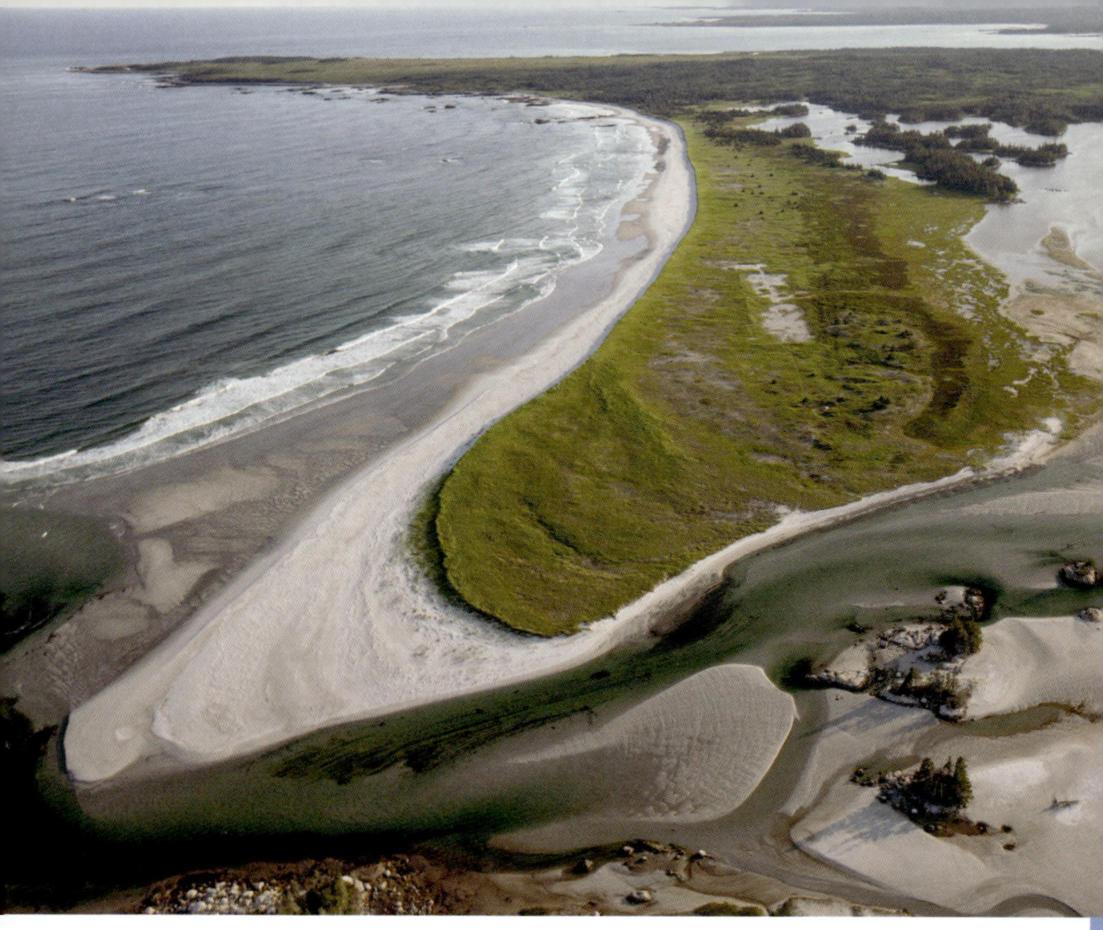

ABOVE ⁓ The Kejimkujik Seaside Adjunct, which is located on the Atlantic coast near Port Joli, is part of Kejimkujik National Park.

FACING ⁓ Bridgewater, located on the LaHave River, is the largest community on Nova Scotia's South Shore.

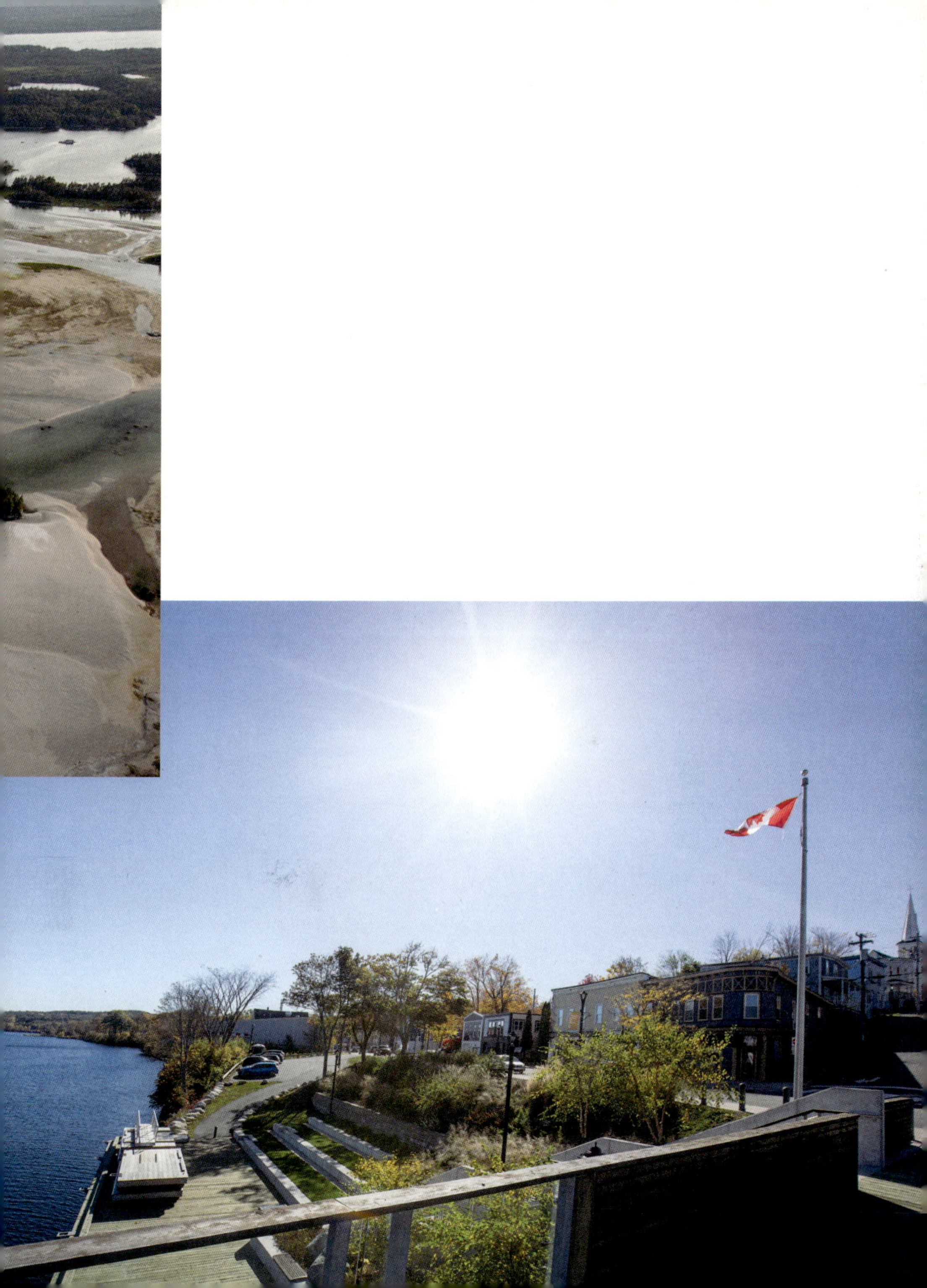

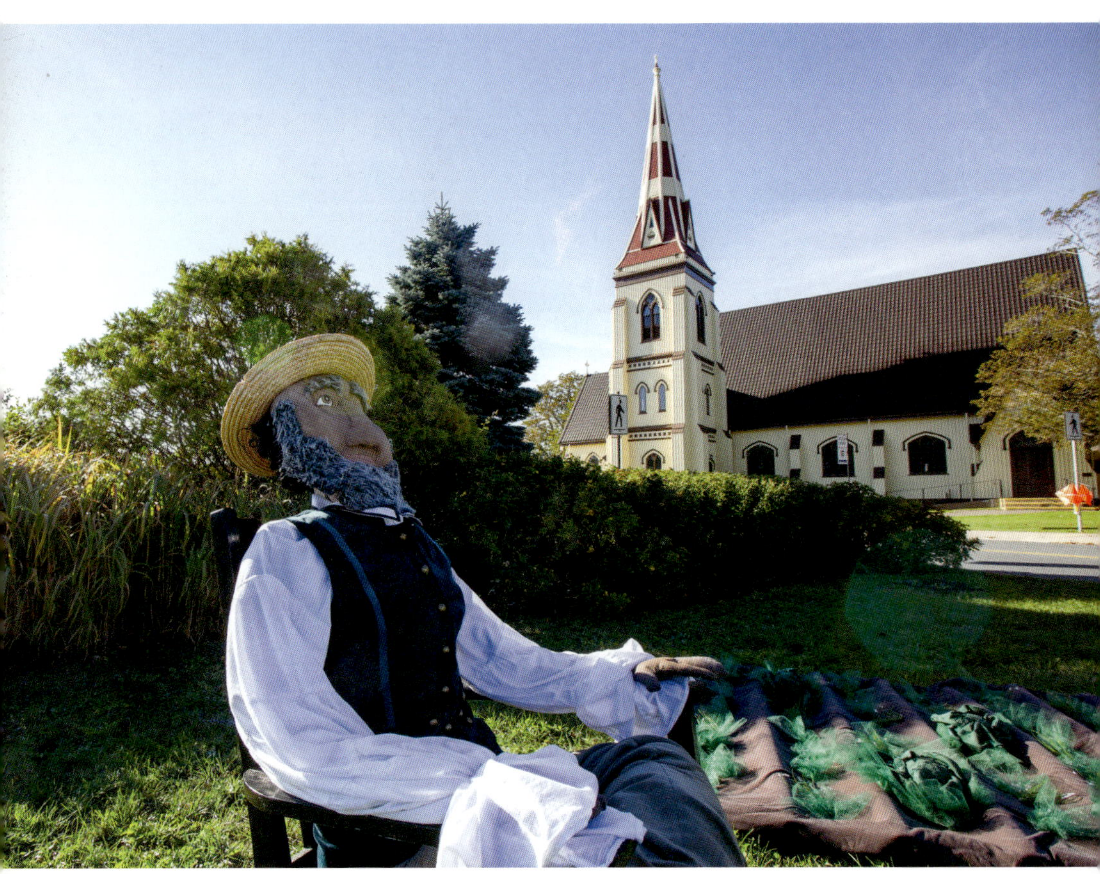

ABOVE ⁓ Mahone Bay's annual Scarecrow Festival in September has been drawing people to the town for nearly twenty-five years.

FACING ⁓ The still waters of Mahone Bay reflect moored boats as the town's iconic waterfront churches stand tall across the bay.

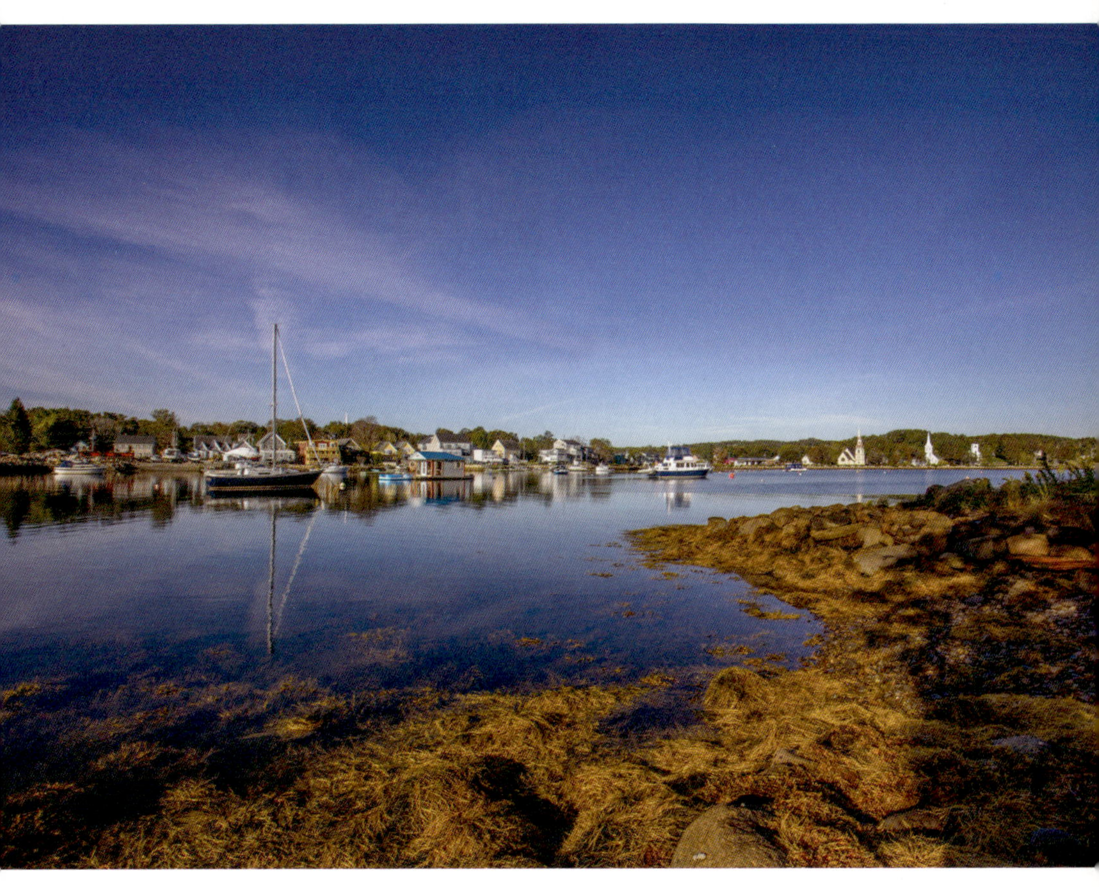

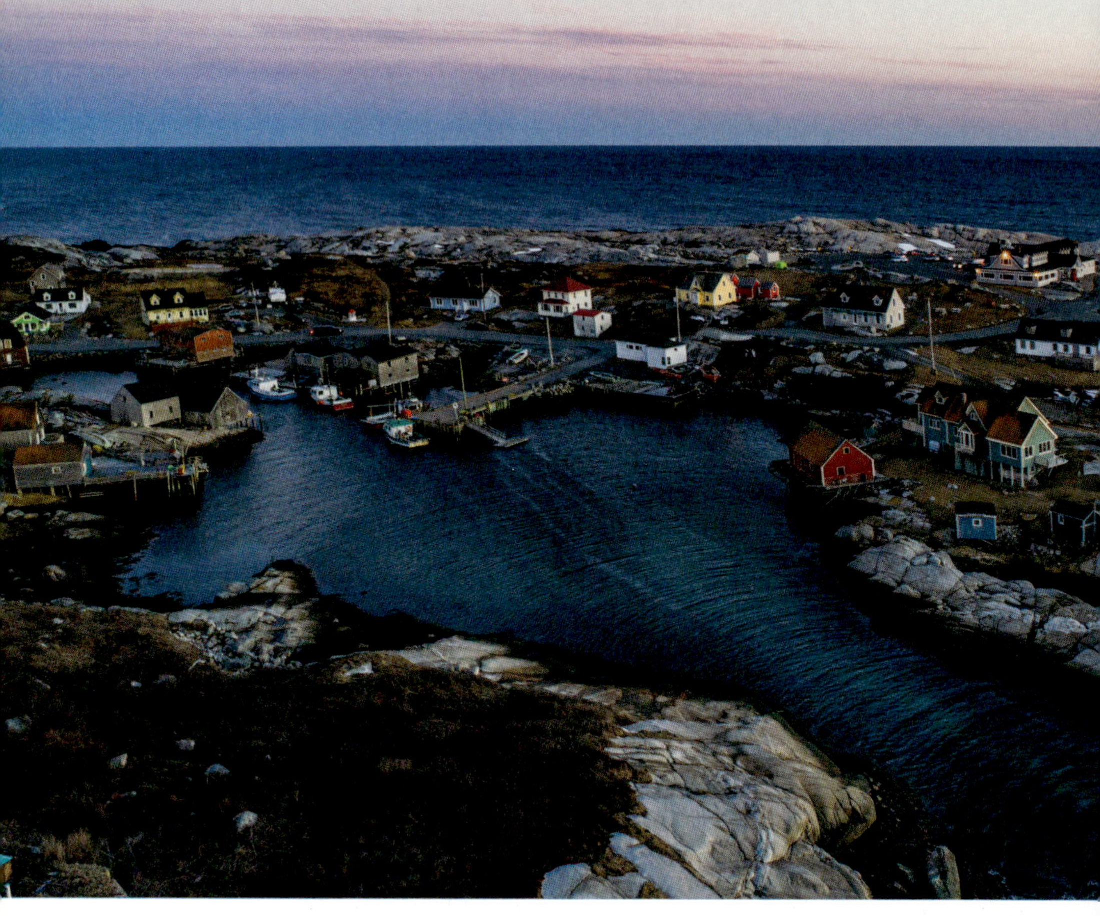

ABOVE ⁓ A cotton-candy sky lingers as twilight falls over Peggys Cove.

FACING ⁓ The colours of fall explode along the Bridgewater riverfront.

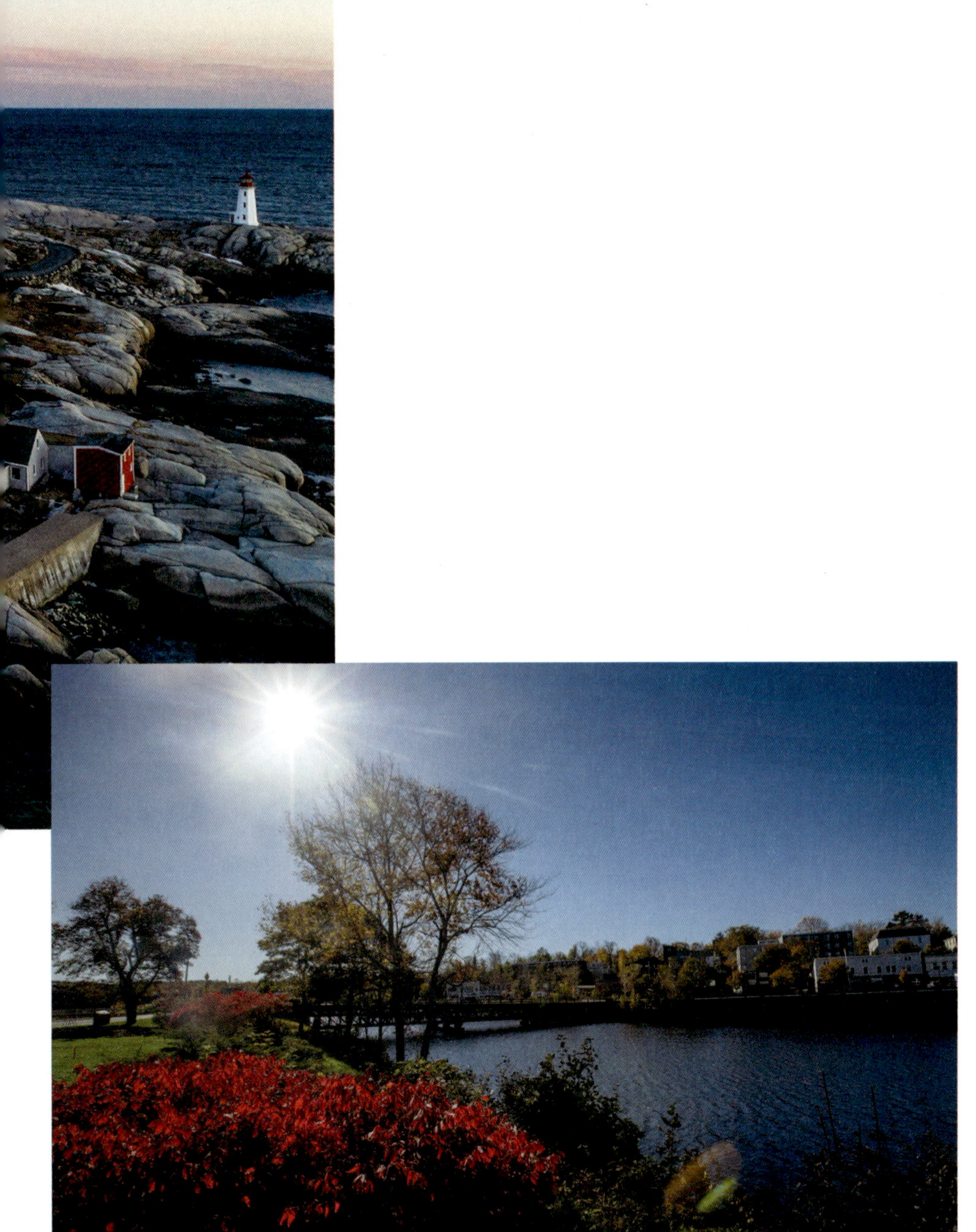

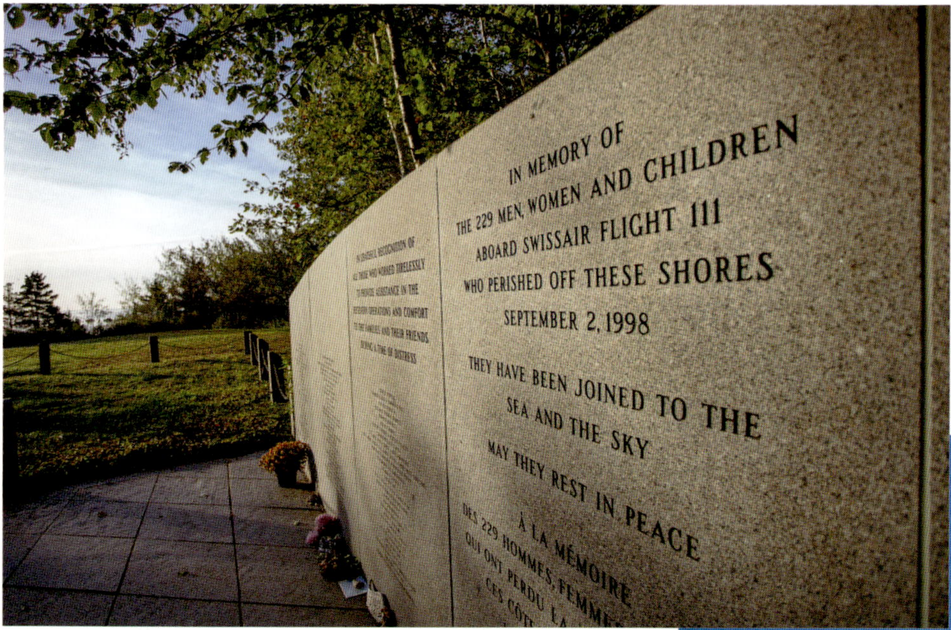

ABOVE ⁓ On the night of September 2, 1998, Swissair Flight 111 crashed into the ocean off Peggys Cove, killing all on board. Hundreds of volunteers spent the following weeks searching for debris, and offering aid to family members who came to mourn at the site where their loved ones had perished.

FACING ⁓ Waves blend together in a long exposure taken on a stormy evening off Peggys Cove.

OVERLEAF ⁓ The picturesque village of Chester draws sailors and visitors from all over the world for its annual Race Week.

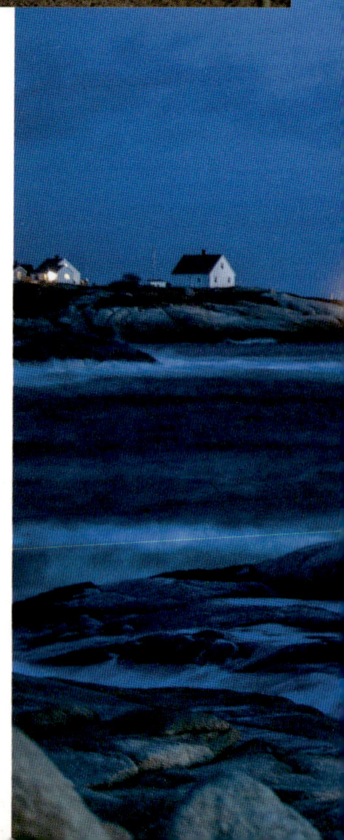

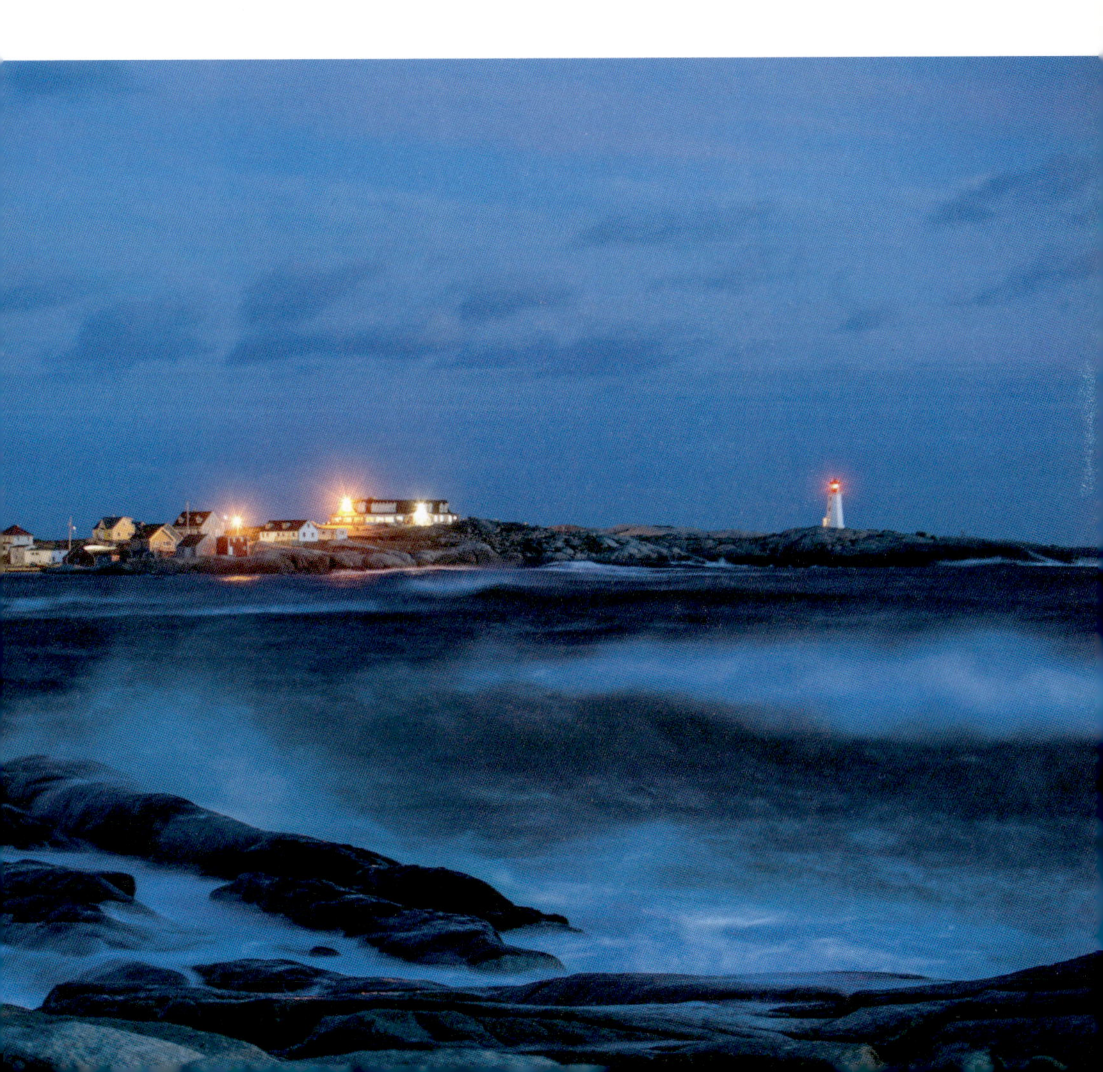

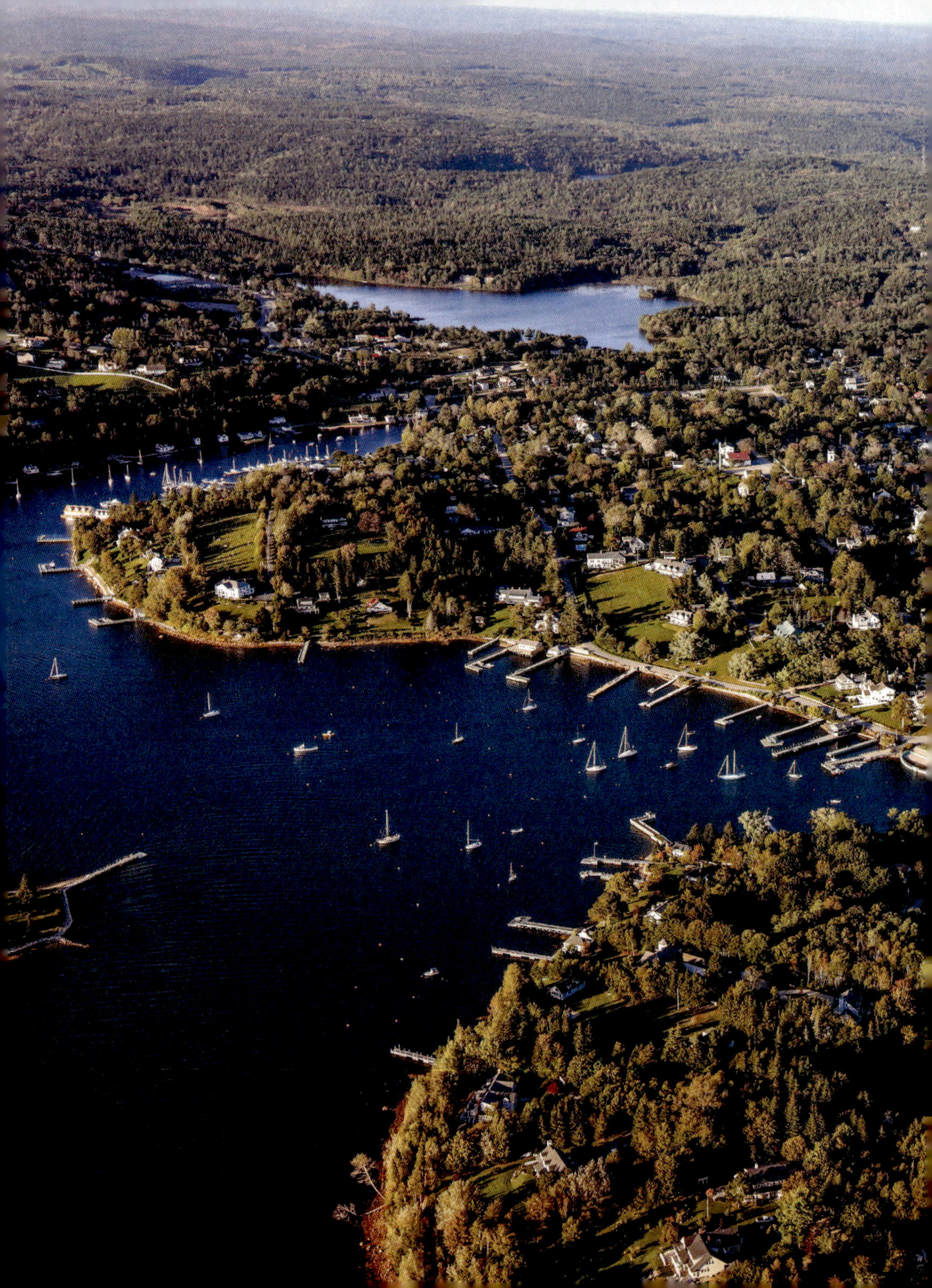

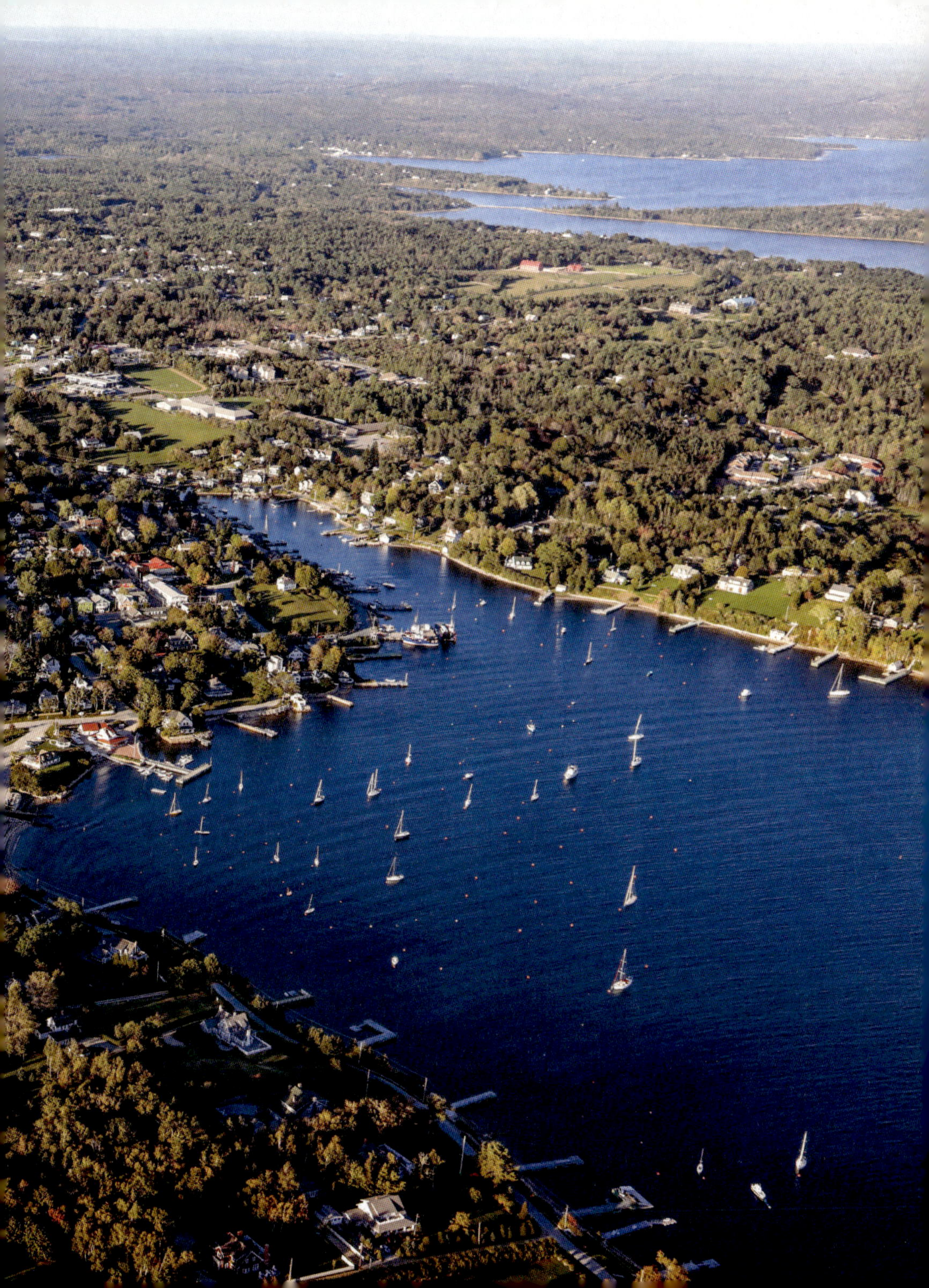

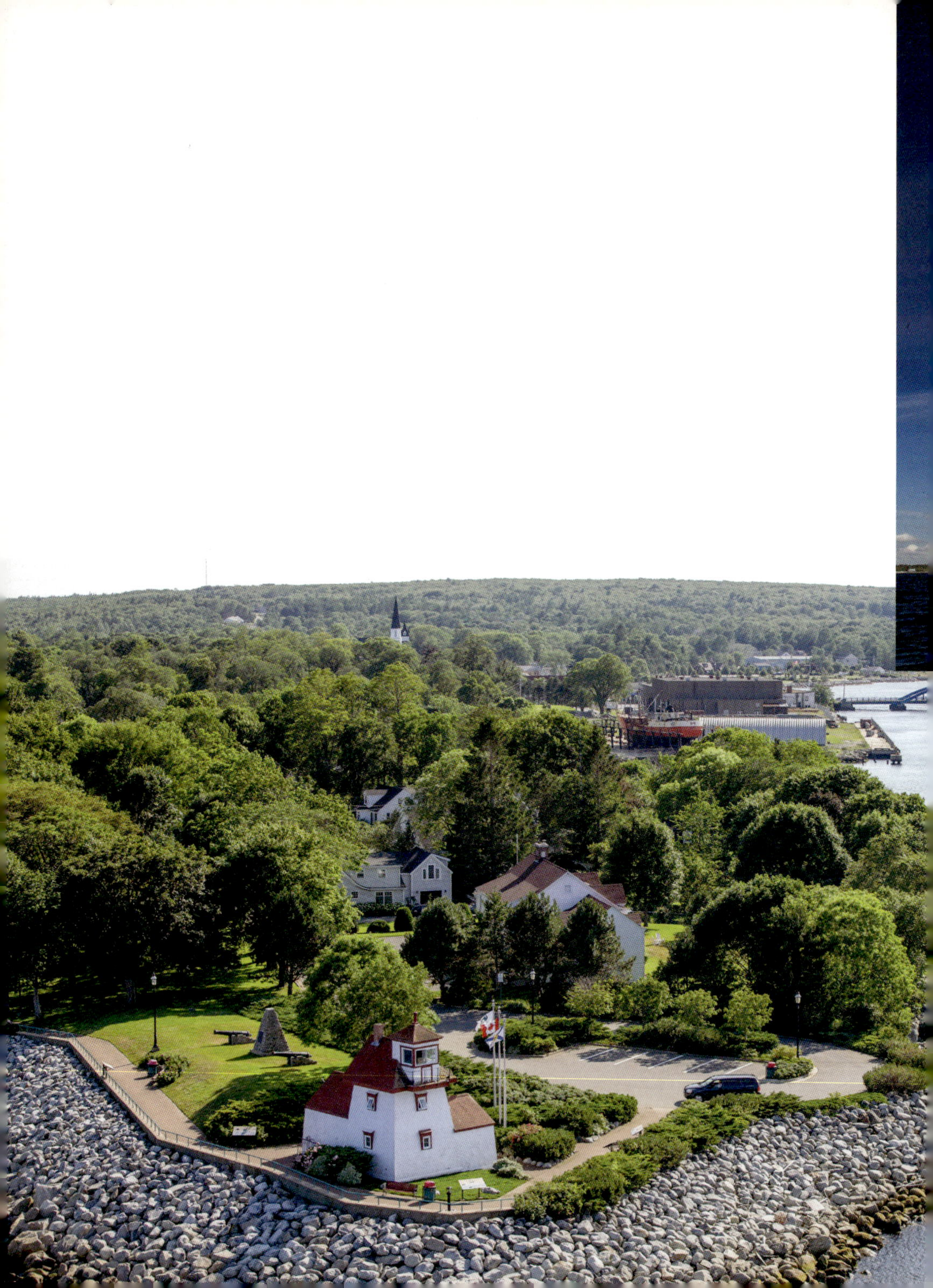

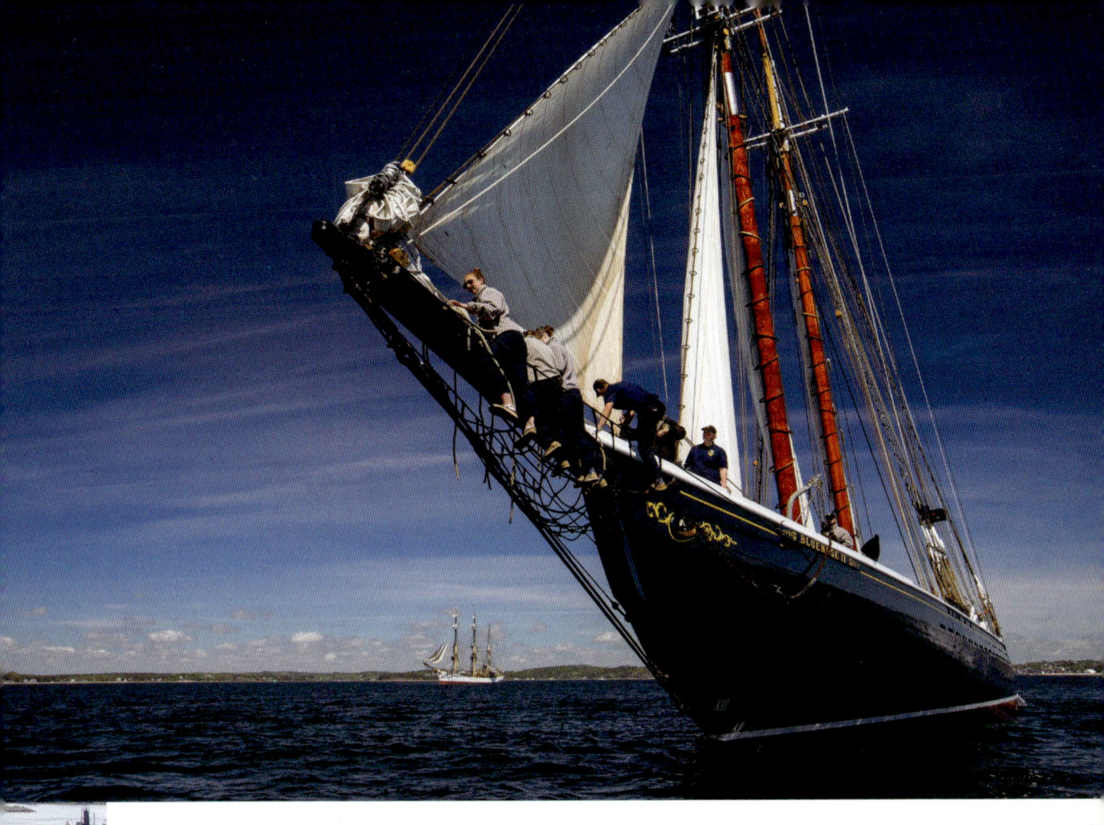

ABOVE ⁓ Crew members aboard *Bluenose II* adjust the jib from the bowsprit of the 43.6-metre vessel, which is Nova Scotia's sailing ambassador.

FACING ⁓ Like many communities on the South Shore, Liverpool is home to numerous descendants of Loyalists who left the United States after the American Revolutionary War.

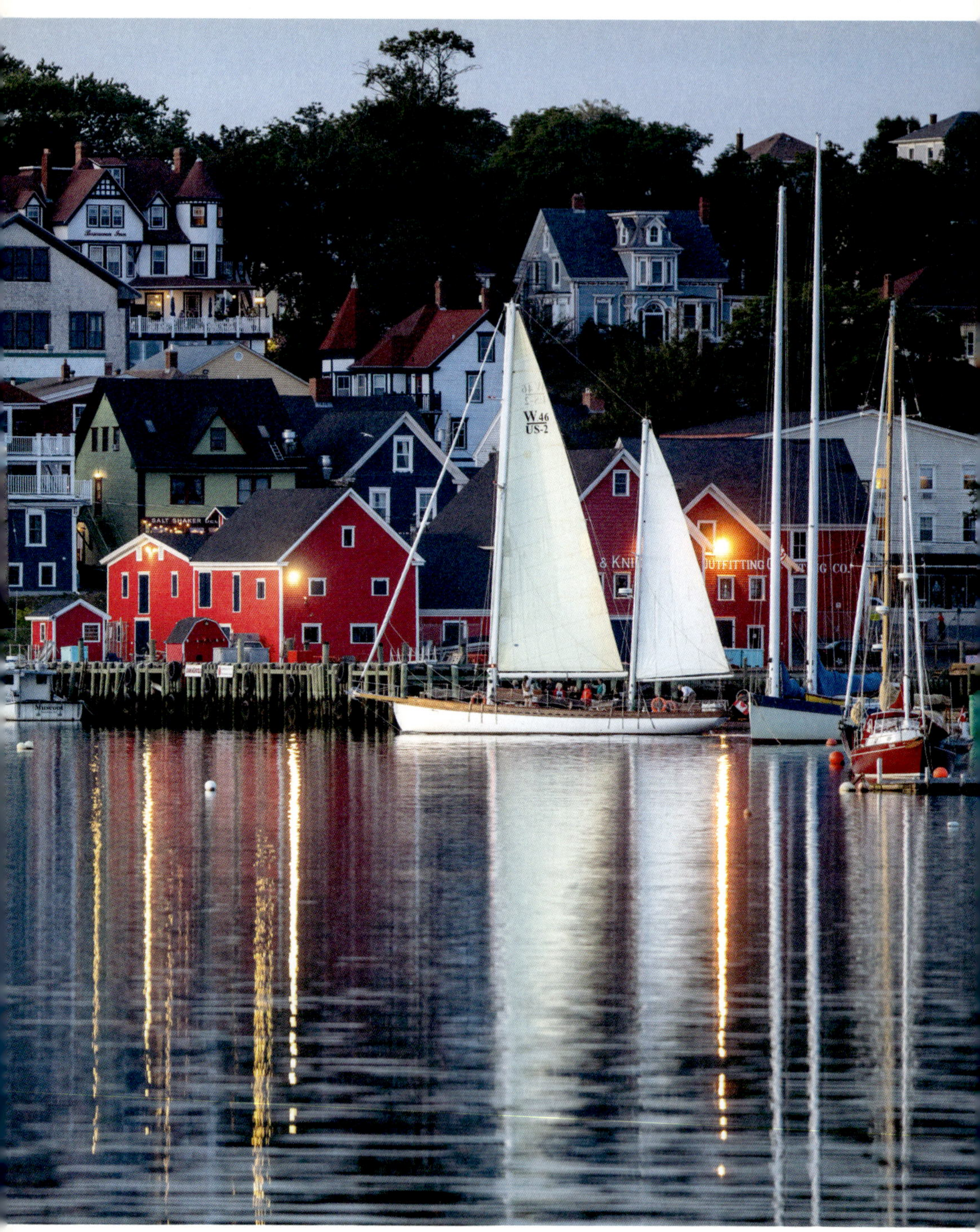
W46
US-2

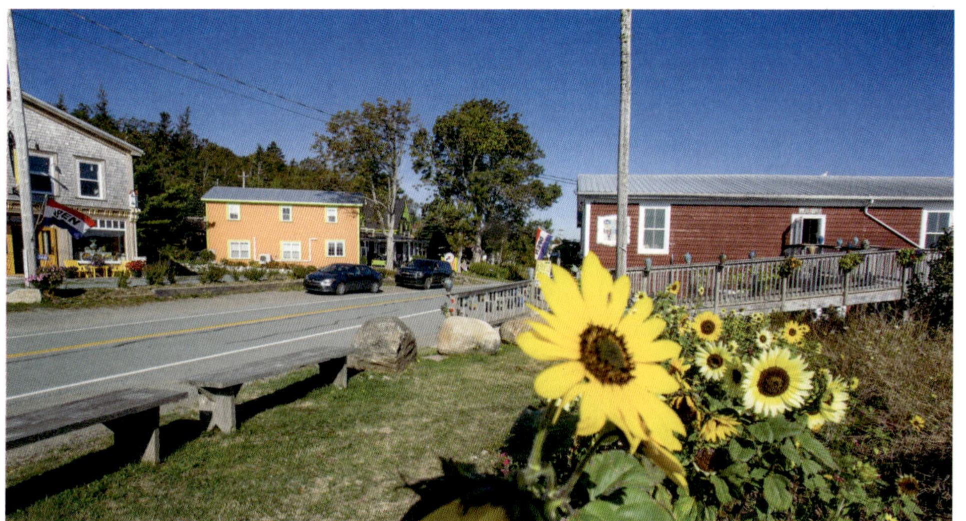

ABOVE ⁓ The LaHave Bakery (left), is a popular lunch spot for those visiting the South Shore.

FACING ⁓ Visitors can admire Lunenburg's colourful waterfront in many ways—including on a sailing tour aboard the *Eastern Star*, shown here.

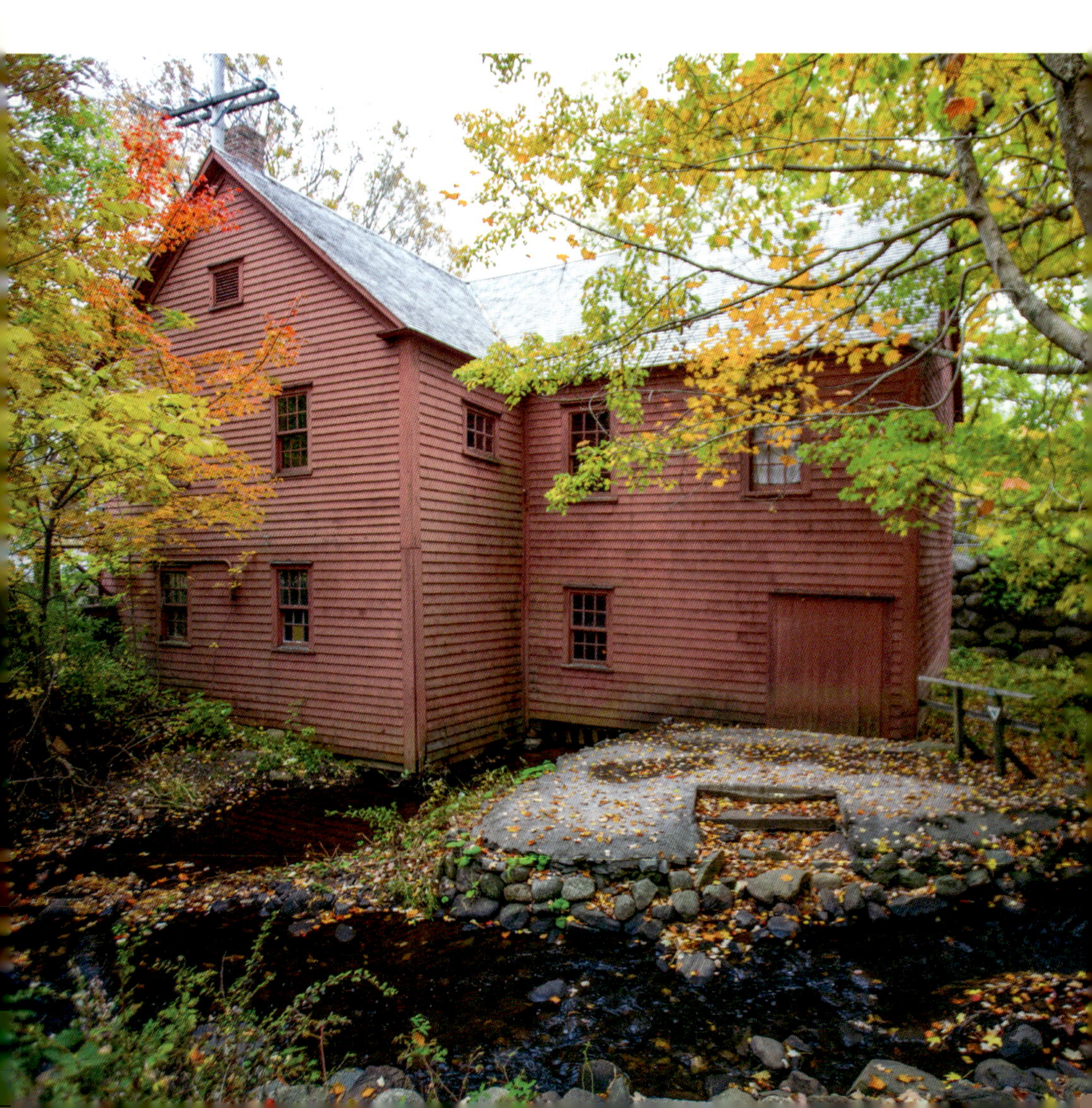

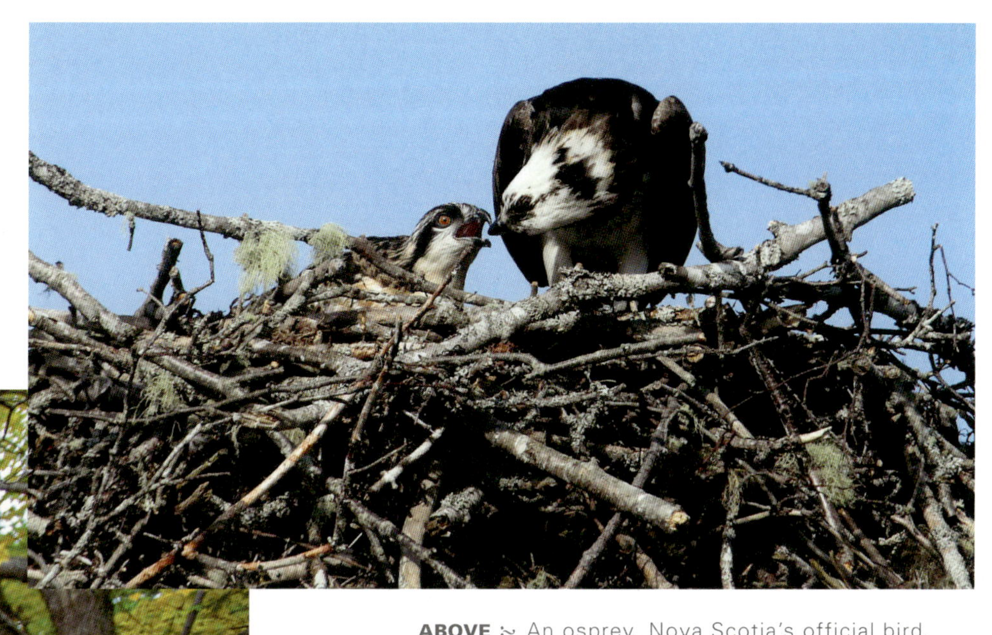

ABOVE ⁓ An osprey, Nova Scotia's official bird, feeds a chick in a huge nest. Ospreys often return to the same nest to raise their young year after year.

FACING ⁓ The Wile Carding Mill Museum in Bridgewater, which operated from 1860 to 1968, was able to card a week's worth of wool in just one hour. Today it operates as a museum.

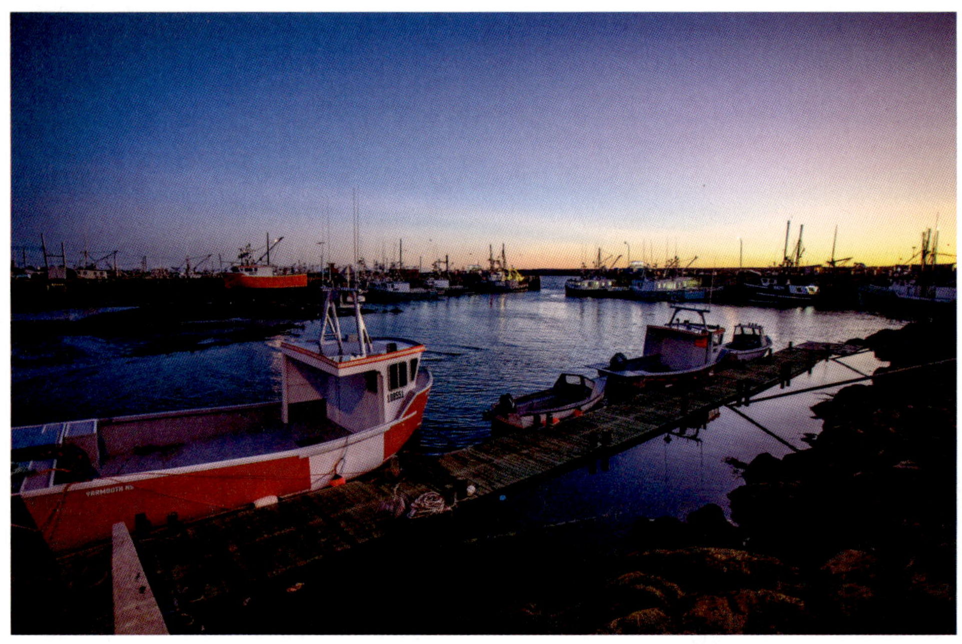

ABOVE ⁓ Dawn lights the sky over the fishing fleet at the Dennis Point wharf in Pubnico.

FACING ⁓ Gulls start their day searching for food as the morning light appears over the Peggys Point Lighthouse.

OVERLEAF ⁓ A sailboat on St. Margarets Bay heads for port in the dying light of the day.

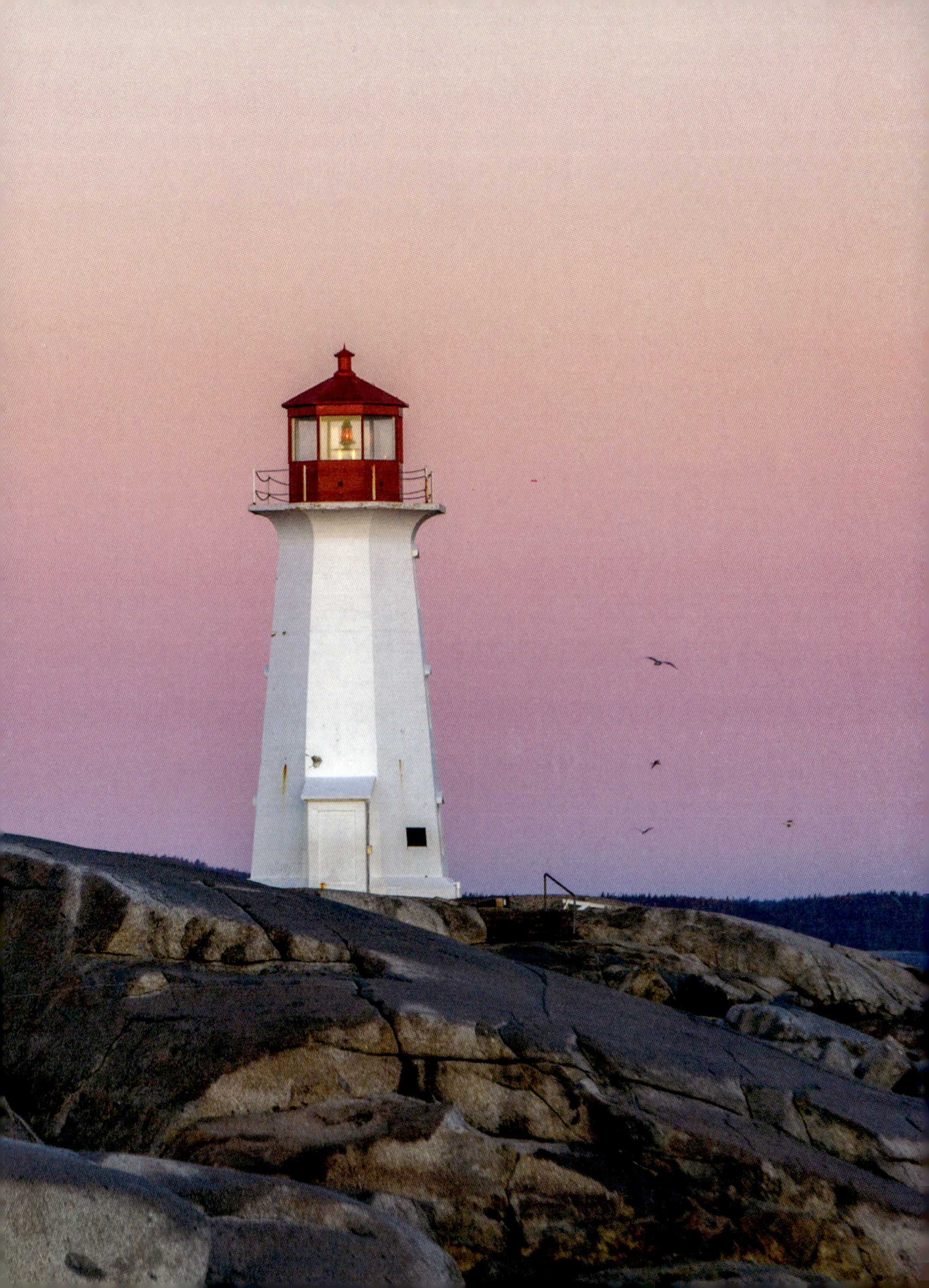

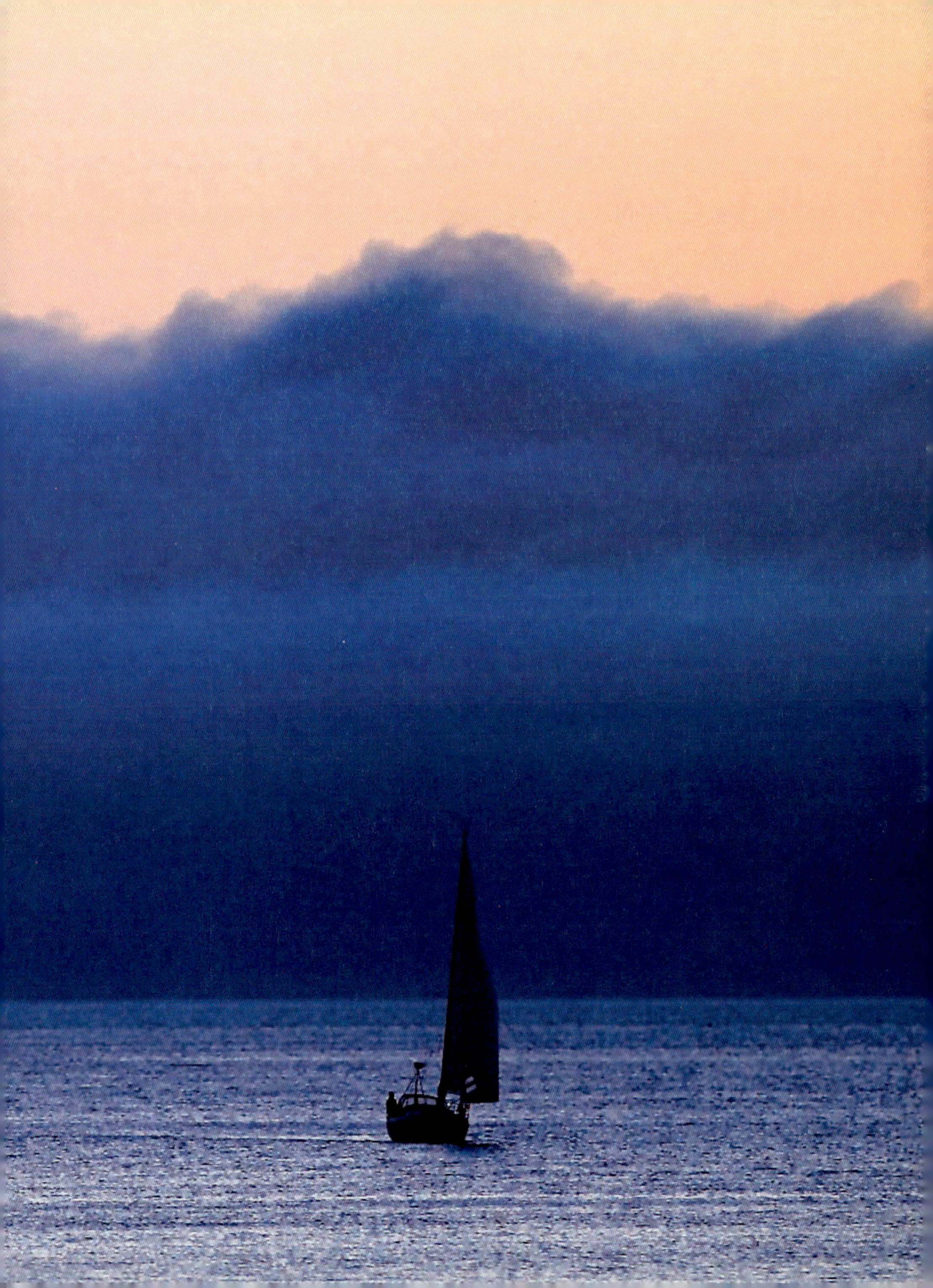

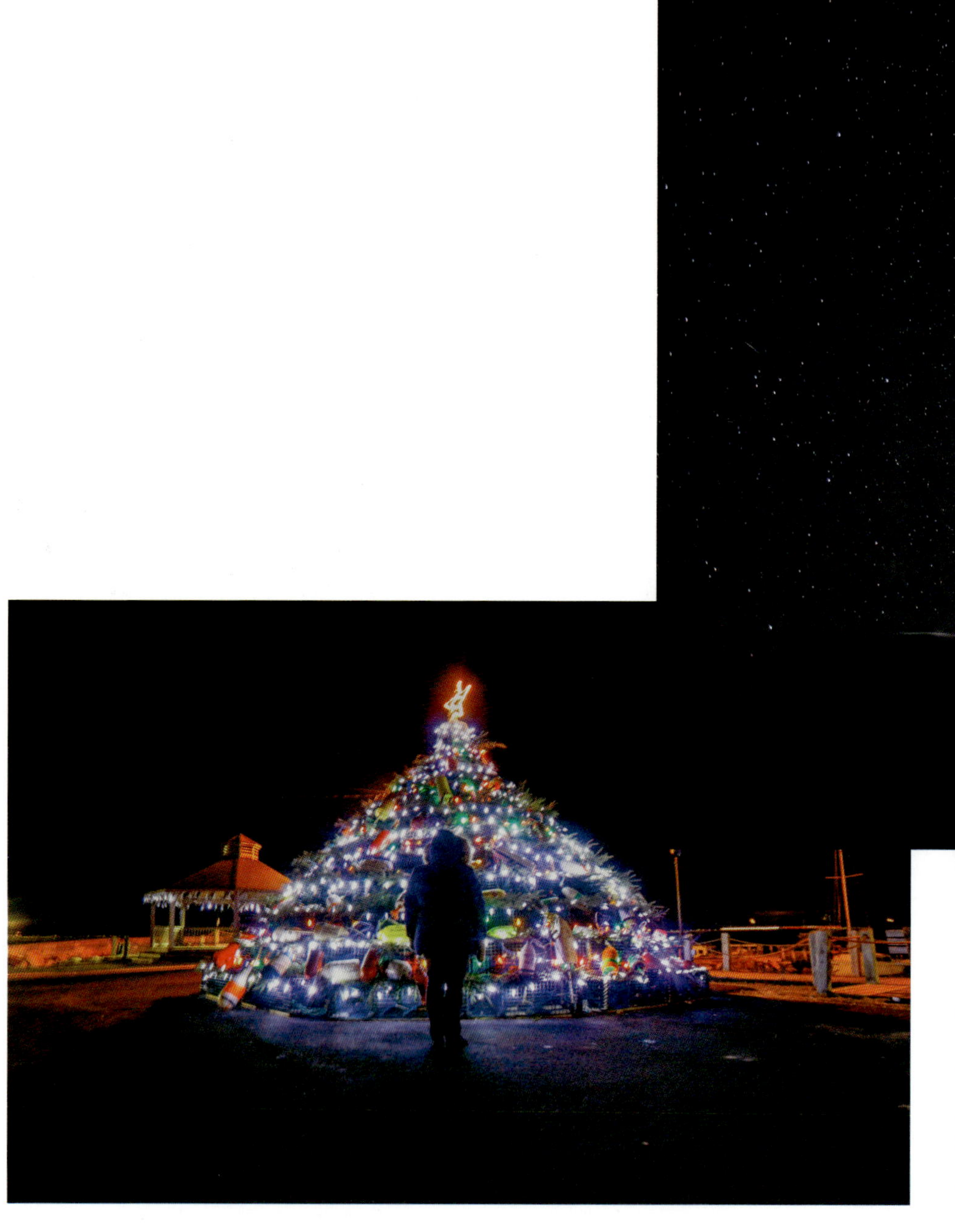

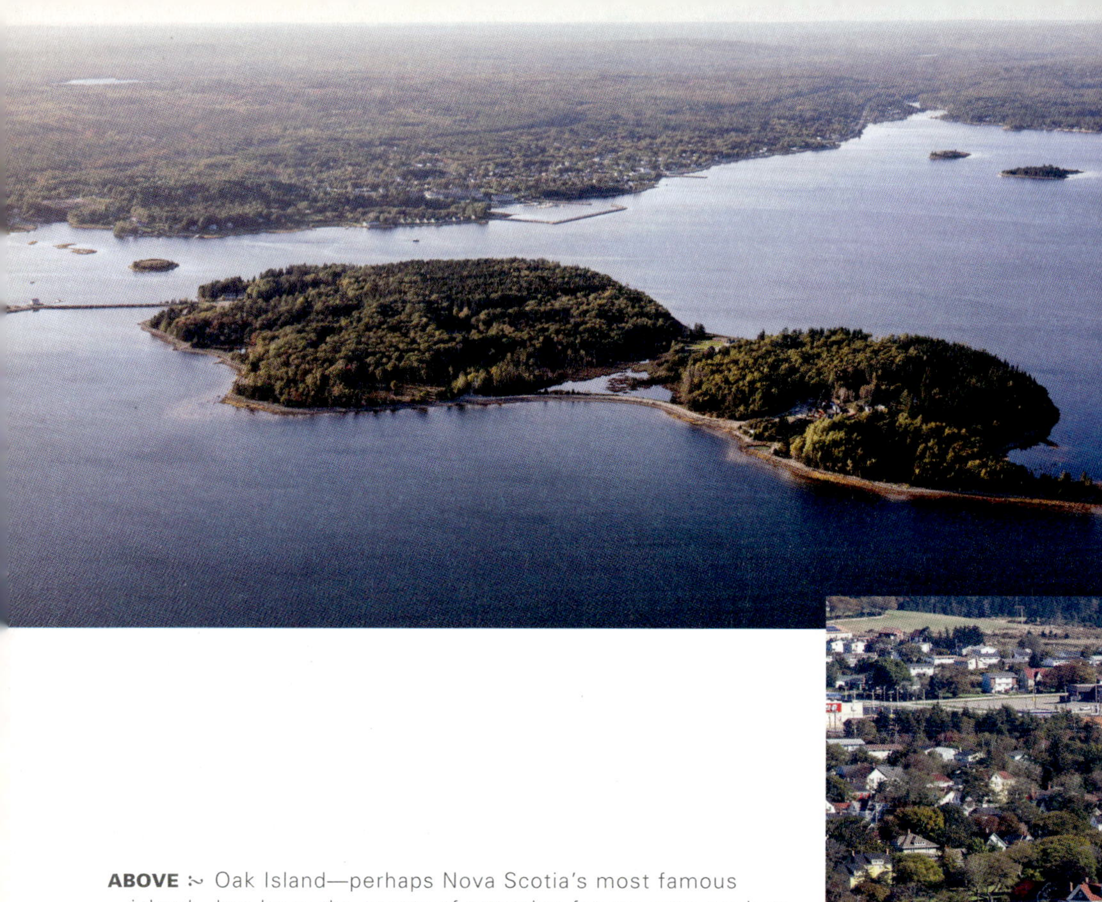

ABOVE ~ Oak Island—perhaps Nova Scotia's most famous island—has been the centre of attention for treasure-seekers since the late 1700s. After hundreds of years of digging, and millions of dollars spent, the treasure remains elusive.

FACING ~ Located at the southwestern tip of the province, Yarmouth has been an important fishing community for hundreds of years.

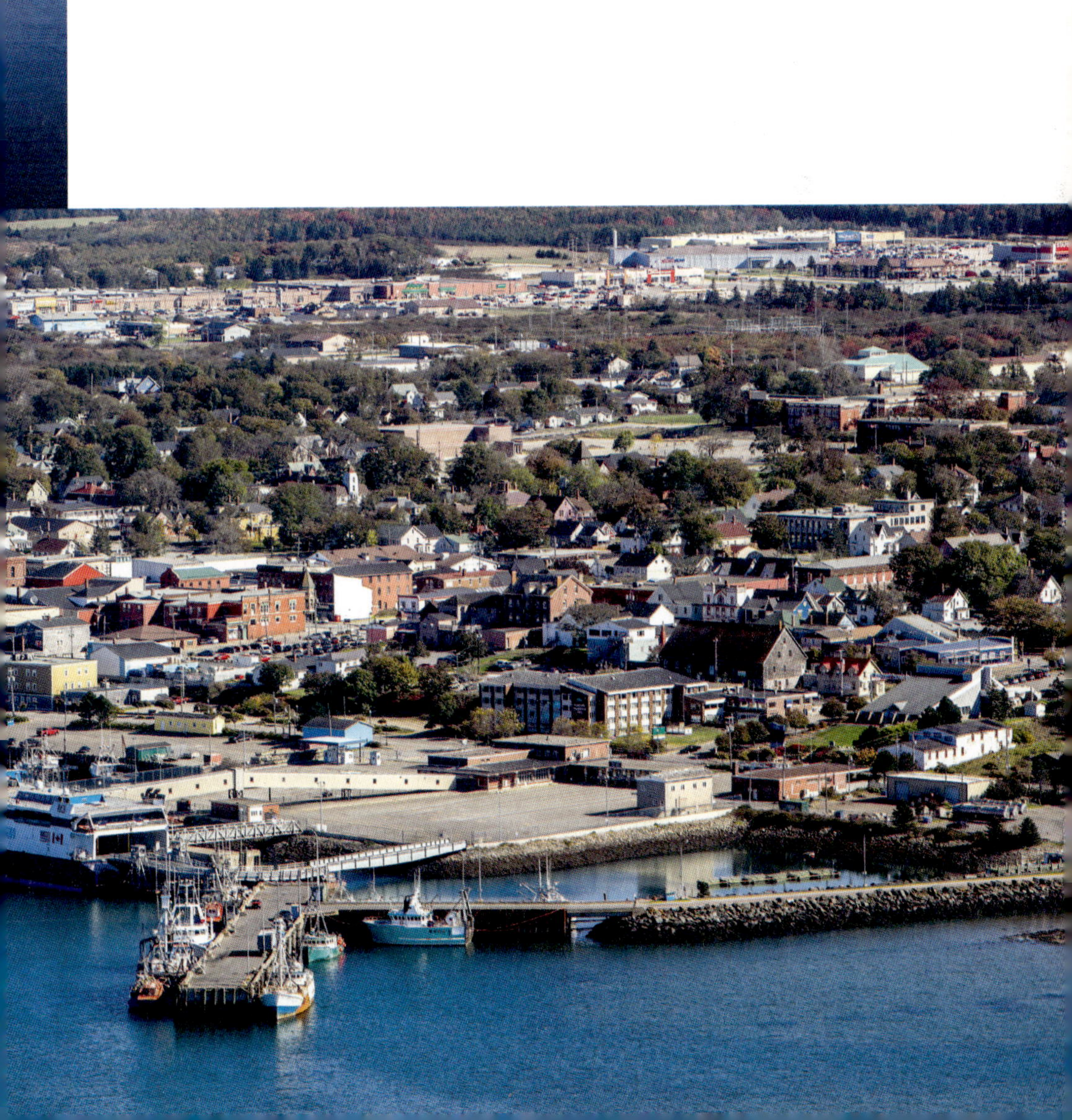

BELOW :~ Tourists enjoy the last rays of sunlight at Peggys Point Lighthouse.

FACING :~ Buoys are piled and ready for the start of the lobster fishing season. Each fisher paints his or her numbered buoys a different colour. Nova Scotia's lobster industry is worth over half a billion dollars.

OVERLEAF :~ The patchwork of islands off the tiny community of Blue Rocks. The many channels make it a fascinating place for a morning paddle.

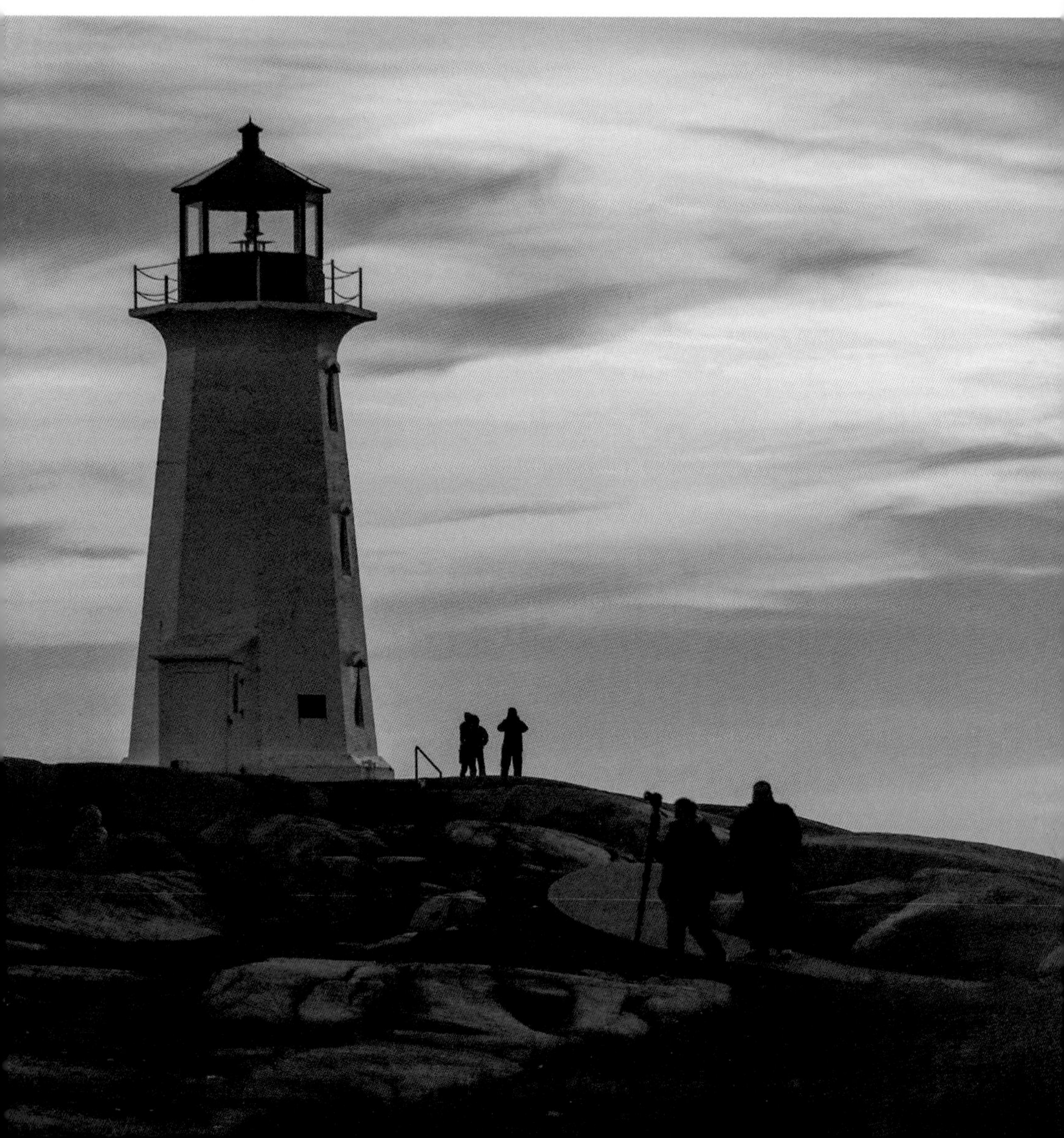

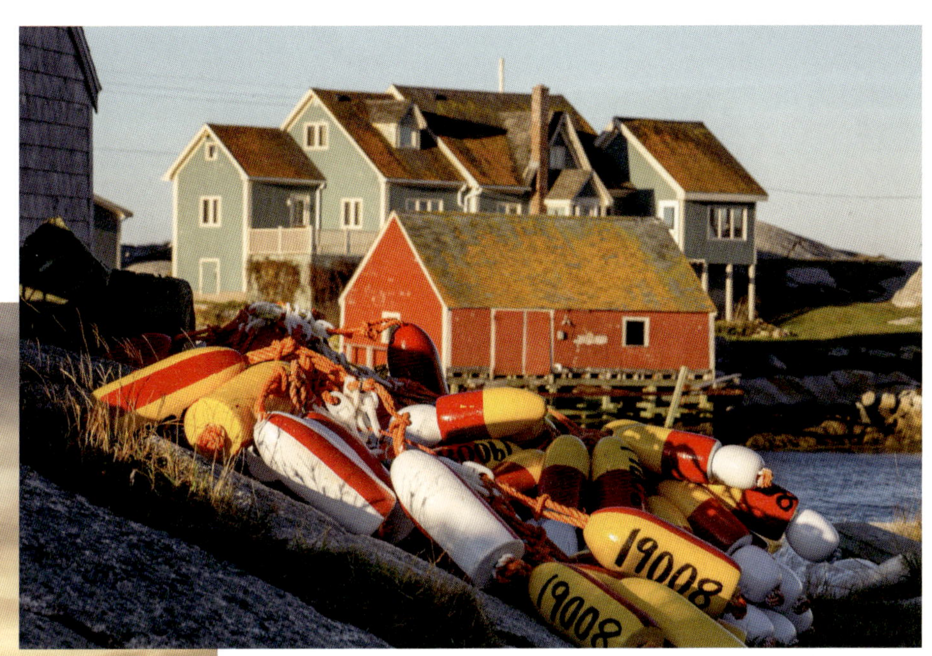
19008
19008

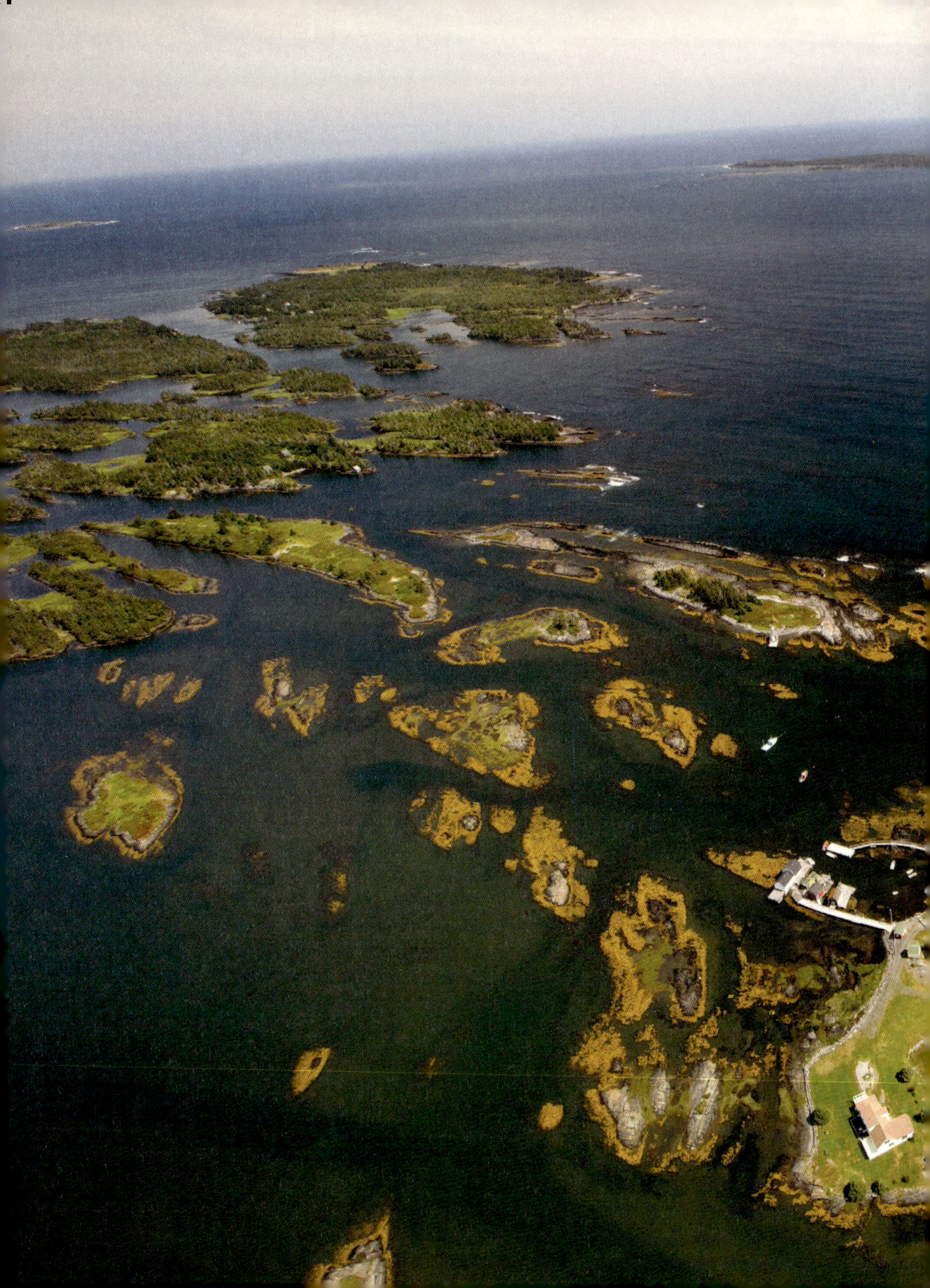

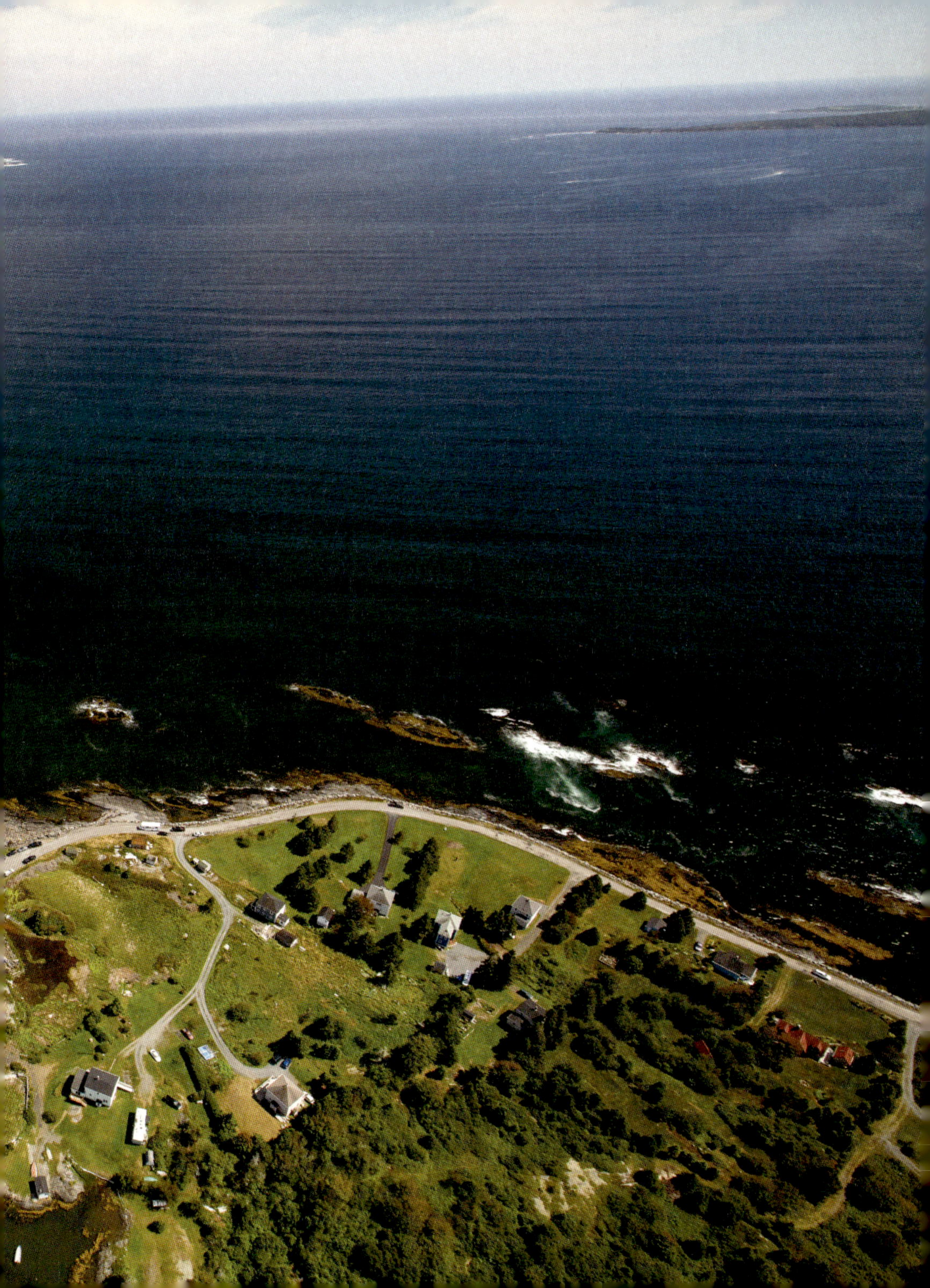

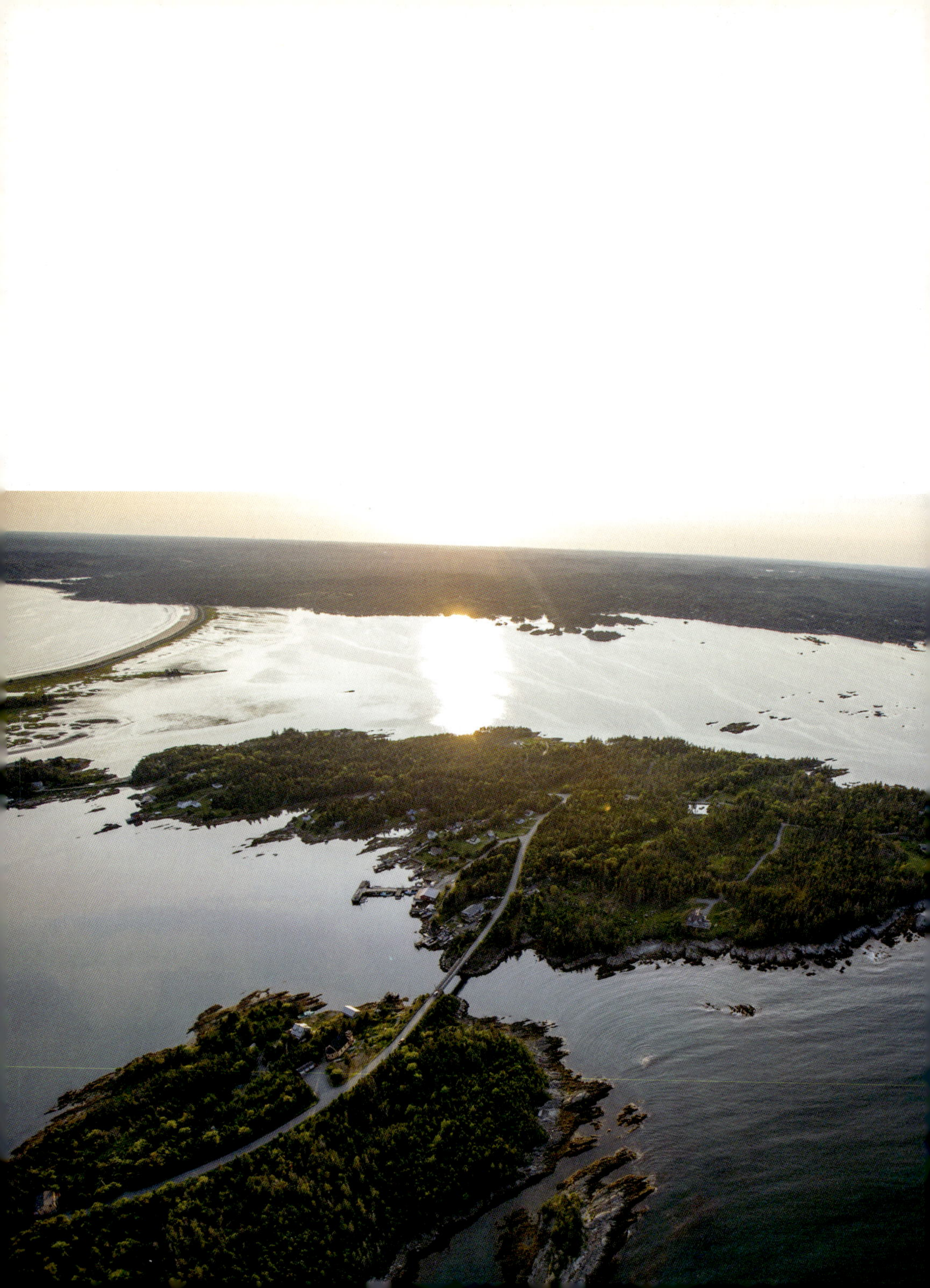

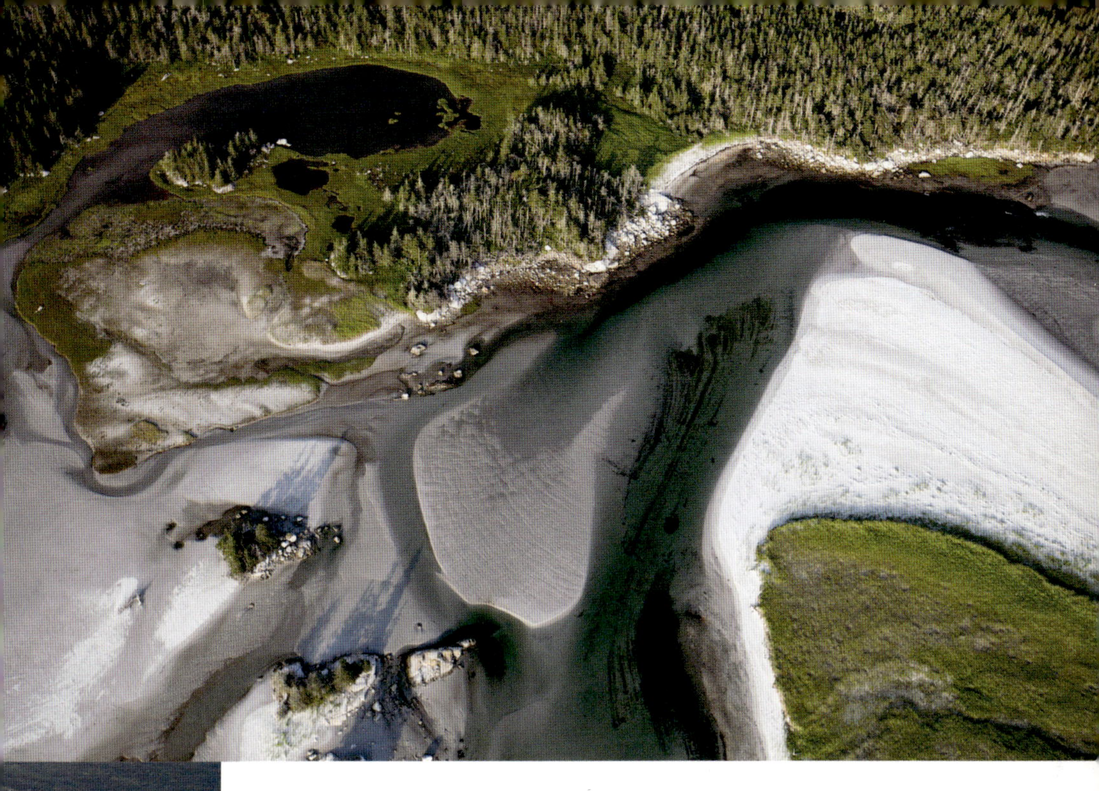

ABOVE ⁓ The sea at the Kejimkujik Seaside Adjunct has an almost-tropical appearance.

FACING ⁓ Bell Island and Bush Island are seen in the foreground as the sun sets behind Crescent Beach.

OVERLEAF ⁓ A lighthouse has stood since 1839 at the opening of Yarmouth Harbour at Cape Forchu. The present-day lighthouse is a popular destination, and the site offers an excellent opportunity for visitors to enjoy an evening of stargazing.

LAST PAGE ⁓ The rising sun illuminates the rocky coastline behind the Peggys Point Lighthouse.

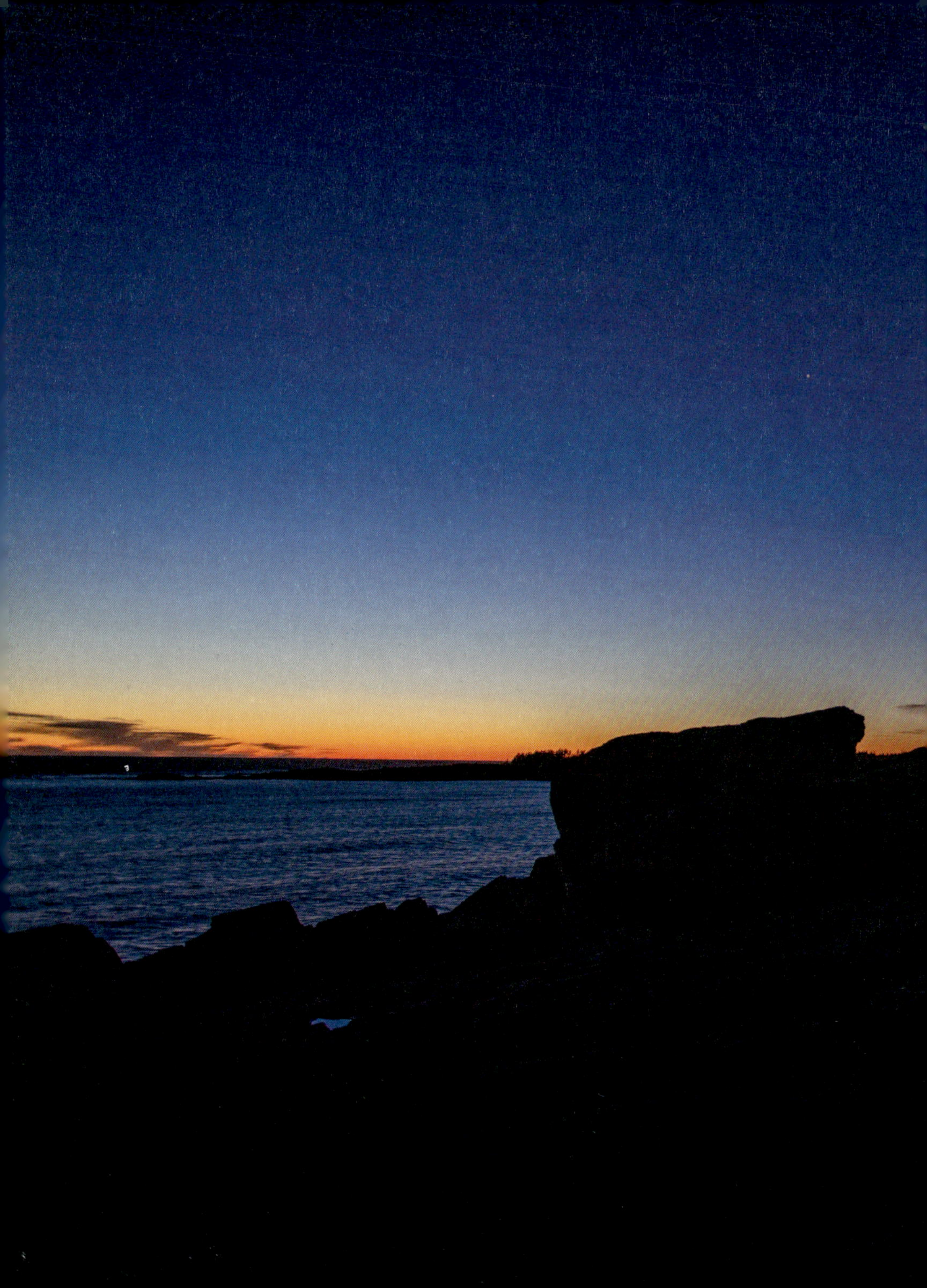

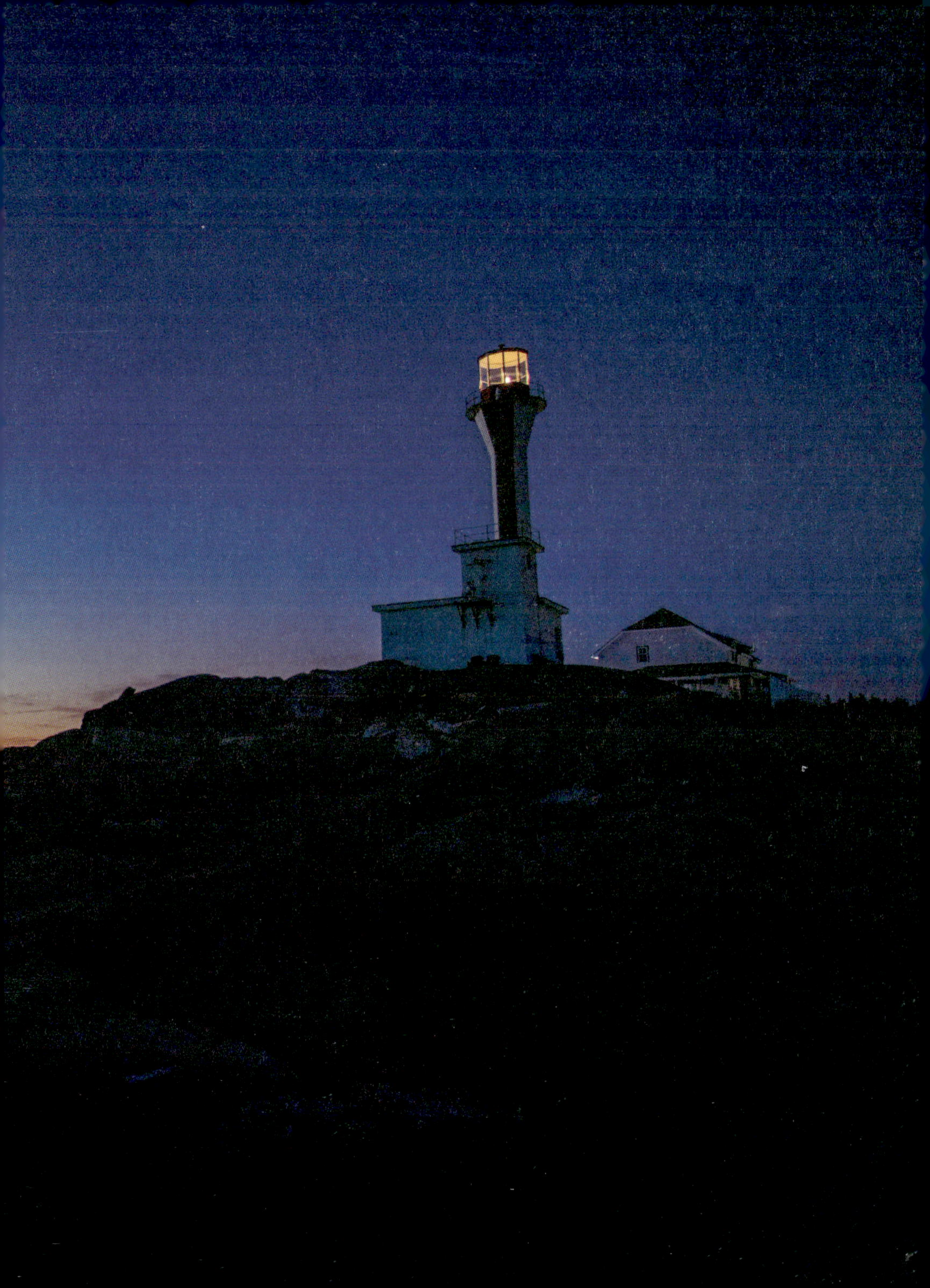

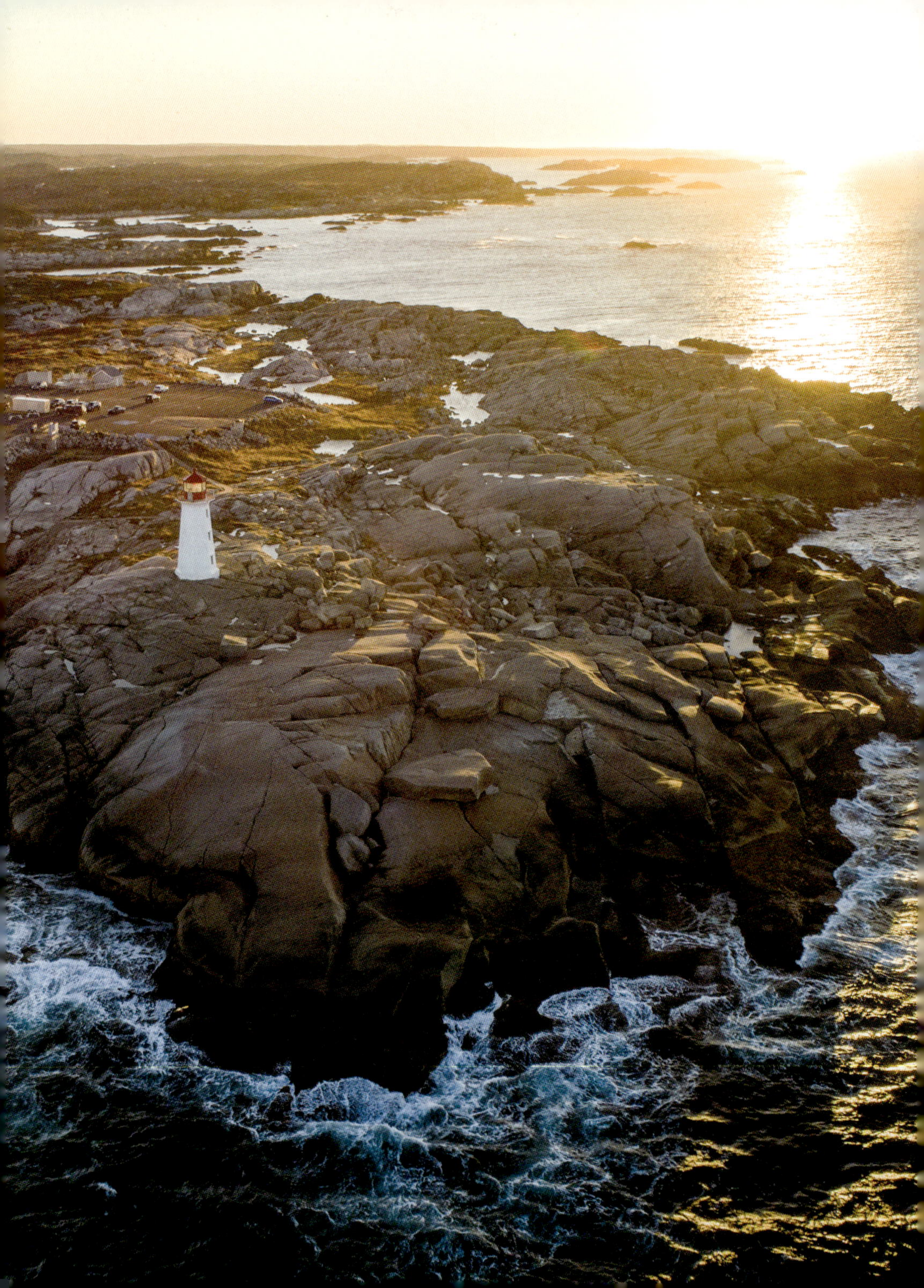